Consumer Debt

Other Books in the Current Controversies Series

CONTROVERSIES

DISCARDED

Consumer Debt

Joseph Tardiff, Book Editor

GREENHAVEN PRESS
A part of Gale, Cengage Learning

GALE
CENGAGE Learning™

Detroit • New York • San Francisco • New Haven, Conn • Waterville, Maine • London

GALE
CENGAGE Learning™

Christine Nasso, *Publisher*
Elizabeth Des Chenes, *Managing Editor*

© 2010 Greenhaven Press, a part of Gale, Cengage Learning

Gale and Greenhaven Press are registered trademarks used herein under license.

For more information, contact:
Greenhaven Press
27500 Drake Rd.
Farmington Hills, MI 48331-3535
Or you can visit our Internet site at gale.cengage.com

For product information and technology assistance, contact us at

Gale Customer Support, 1-800-877-4253
For permission to use material from this text or product, submit all requests online at www.cengage.com/permissions

Further permissions questions can be emailed to permissionrequest@cengage.com

Articles in Greenhaven Press anthologies are often edited for length to meet page requirements. In addition, original titles of these works are changed to clearly present the main thesis and to explicitly indicate the author's opinion. Every effort is made to ensure that Greenhaven Press accurately reflects the original intent of the authors. Every effort has been made to trace the owners of copyrighted material.

Cover image copyright © Tammy Hanratty/Fancy/Corbis.

LIBRARY OF CONGRESS CATALOGING-IN-PUBLICATION DATA

Consumer debt / Joseph Tardiff, book editor.
    p. cm. -- (Current controversies)
    Includes bibliographical references and index.
    ISBN 978-0-7377-4701-0 (hardcover) -- ISBN 978-0-7377-4702-7 (pbk.)
  1. Consumer credit--juvenile literature. I. Tardiff, Joseph C., 1966-
  HG3755.C588 2010
  332.7'43--dc22

                                                               2009048658

Printed in the United States of America
1 2 3 4 5 6 7 14 13 12 11 10

Contents

Chapter 4: Is Declaring Bankruptcy a Good Way to Handle Too Much Debt?

Foreword

By definition, controversies are "discussions of questions in which opposing opinions clash" (Webster's Twentieth Century Dictionary Unabridged). Few would deny that controversies are a pervasive part of the human condition and exist on virtually every level of human enterprise. Controversies transpire between individuals and among groups, within nations and between nations. Controversies supply the grist necessary for progress by providing challenges and challengers to the status quo. They also create atmospheres where strife and warfare can flourish. A world without controversies would be a peaceful world; but it also would be, by and large, static and prosaic.

The Series' Purpose

The purpose of the Current Controversies series is to explore many of the social, political, and economic controversies dominating the national and international scenes today. Titles selected for inclusion in the series are highly focused and specific. For example, from the larger category of criminal justice, Current Controversies deals with specific topics such as police brutality, gun control, white collar crime, and others. The debates in Current Controversies also are presented in a useful, timeless fashion. Articles and book excerpts included in each title are selected if they contribute valuable, long-range ideas to the overall debate. And wherever possible, current information is enhanced with historical documents and other relevant materials. Thus, while individual titles are current in focus, every effort is made to ensure that they will not become quickly outdated. Books in the Current Controversies series will remain important resources for librarians, teachers, and students for many years.

In addition to keeping the titles focused and specific, great care is taken in the editorial format of each book in the series. Book introductions and chapter prefaces are offered to provide background material for readers. Chapters are organized around several key questions that are answered with diverse opinions representing all points on the political spectrum. Materials in each chapter include opinions in which authors clearly disagree as well as alternative opinions in which authors may agree on a broader issue but disagree on the possible solutions. In this way, the content of each volume in Current Controversies mirrors the mosaic of opinions encountered in society. Readers will quickly realize that there are many viable answers to these complex issues. By questioning each author's conclusions, students and casual readers can begin to develop the critical thinking skills so important to evaluating opinionated material.

Current Controversies is also ideal for controlled research. Each anthology in the series is composed of primary sources taken from a wide gamut of informational categories including periodicals, newspapers, books, U.S. and foreign government documents, and the publications of private and public organizations. Readers will find factual support for reports, debates, and research papers covering all areas of important issues. In addition, an annotated table of contents, an index, a book and periodical bibliography, and a list of organizations to contact are included in each book to expedite further research.

Perhaps more than ever before in history, people are confronted with diverse and contradictory information. During the Persian Gulf War, for example, the public was not only treated to minute-to-minute coverage of the war, it was also inundated with critiques of the coverage and countless analyses of the factors motivating U.S. involvement. Being able to sort through the plethora of opinions accompanying today's major issues, and to draw one's own conclusions, can be a complicated and frustrating struggle. It is the editors' hope that Current Controversies will help readers with this struggle.

Introduction

"The global financial meltdown ... ushered in a new era of fiscal circumspection on the part of financiers and consumers alike."

On May 22, 2009, President Barack Obama signed into law the Credit Card Accountability, Responsibility, and Disclosure (CARD) Act. This legislation is designed to protect American consumers from what many believe to be unfair and deceptive lending practices on the part of the credit card services industry. It is hoped that the reform measures outlined in the CARD Act will offset years of shared fiscal irresponsibility, during which credit card companies unscrupulously extended credit to high-risk borrowers and credulous consumers took advantage of easy credit terms to run up excessive credit card debt. The legislation also capitalizes on the economic fallout from the global financial meltdown of 2008, which ushered in a new era of fiscal circumspection on the part of financiers and consumers alike. Upon signing the bill, Obama issued a White House press release, stating that "With this new law, consumers will have the strong and reliable protections they deserve. We will continue to press for reform that is built on transparency, accountability, and mutual responsibility—values fundamental to the new foundation we seek to build for our economy."

The CARD Act will be phased in gradually between 2009 and 2010. The first round of rules takes effect in August 2009. Credit card companies must give cardholders written notice forty-five days prior to increasing interest rates or making changes to account terms—an increase from the current fifteen day period. In the same notice, credit card companies must inform cardholders that they have the right to cancel their account before the proposed changes take effect; if they exercise this right, cardholders can no longer use the card and they must pay off their existing balance within five years under the original credit terms. In addition, credit card companies must mail cardholders their account statements at least twenty-one days before the payment is due, up from the current fourteen day period.

Even more consumer protections will be rolled out in February 2010. Credit card companies will be required to set account balance due dates on the same day each month; if the due date falls on a weekend or a holiday, the payment is not considered late if it is received on the next business day. Credit card companies must apply payment amounts of more than the minimum to balances with the highest interest rates first. And companies cannot raise interest rates on an existing balance if the cardholder is making monthly payments on time. In addition, credit card companies will be required to offer cardholders the opportunity to alter the terms of their accounts to mitigate the embarrassment of being declined at the point of sale for an over-the-limit transaction. Another rule states that individuals under the age of twenty-one will not be able to open a credit card account unless they can secure a cosigner over the age of twenty-one or they can provide documentation proving that they have an established source of income.

In the months prior to the implementation of the CARD Act, credit card companies adjusted account terms and increased fees for millions of cardholders in an effort to mitigate the effects of the reform measures on their profit margins. Perhaps the biggest change is that many major banks began transferring cardholders from fixed- to variable-rate credit cards. Whereas the CARD Act prohibits credit card companies from raising interest rates on existing balances for fixed-rate cards, there is no such provision for variable-rate cards. In addition to these changes, some credit card companies have preemptively increased interest rates on purchases and cash advances and reduced the grace periods during which cardholders can pay their bills without incurring penalties. Other changes that will likely take effect as a result of the new law include the application of an annual fee to more credit cards, higher fees related to transferring balances from one card to another, an increase in the monthly minimum payment due, and a decrease in rewards and benefits programs.

Given the magnitude of the CARD Act's reforms and the credit card companies' renewed efforts to seek alternative ways to make a profit, consumer advocates urge cardholders to be especially vigilant as the rules of the system begin to change. They recommend that cardholders should carefully study the provisions of the CARD Act in order to gain a clear understanding of their new rights under the law. Cardholders should then shop around for a credit card program that best suits their individual needs. Perhaps most important of all, advocates argue, is that common sense and fiscal prudence should guide one's actions under the new system just as they should have under the old one. As Brad Tuttle points out in *Time* magazine on August 20, 2009, "Don't spend more than you have. You should think of a credit card like a handy, expedient alternative to cash, not as a mini-loan operation."

While many of the credit card companies' preemptive moves have compelled consumers to be even more diligent about managing their credit cards, the CARD Act legislation nevertheless has been hailed as a triumph for consumer rights. Indeed, proponents of the law assert that it will ultimately make the credit card lending and balance repayment process much more transparent, giving financially strapped consumers increased flexibility and better choices when it comes to making monthly payments. As U.S. Senator Jeff Merkley writes in the Oregon *Statesman-Journal* on August 30, 2009, "for too long, unregulated consumer credit practices have been stripping wealth from our families, turning a useful tool into a destructive force. The new CARD Act reforms start restoring balance to our financial system so that it works for the best interests of America's families and America's economy once again."

CHAPTER 1

Is Consumer Debt
Bad for the Economy?

Overview: The Benefits and Pitfalls of Consumer Credit Usage

Kristie M. Engemann and Michael T. Owyang

Kristie M. Engemann is a research analyst and Michael T. Owyang is an economist at the Federal Reserve Bank of St. Louis.

The average American is carrying more debt than ever. According to the 2004 Survey of Consumer Finances (SCF), the percentage of families holding debt rose from 72.3 percent in 1989 to 76.4 percent in 2004. Among families holding debt, the median value of the debt more than doubled during that time from $22,000 to $55,300 (in 2004 dollars). These numbers reflect both a rise in collateralized debt (e.g., mortgages) and uncollateralized debt (e.g., credit cards). During the same period, median family income increased by only 12.8 percent to $43,100.

This shift toward more debt appears to have long-term ramifications for the U.S. economy, as evidenced by the growing number of personal bankruptcies over recent decades. Perhaps playing a role in this rise is the increase in debt accumulated via credit cards and payday loans.

Paper or Plastic?

In 1989, a total of 55.8 percent of American families owned at least one credit card; in 2004, a total of 74.9 percent owned at least one card. Over time, the characteristics of credit card holders have changed to include people who are riskier for the lenders.[1] For example, a higher percentage of single people and renters now have a credit card. Also, workers with less job seniority, lower incomes, and unskilled jobs are now more

Kristie M. Engemann and Michael T. Owyang, "Extra Credit: The Rise of Short-Term Liabilities," *The Regional Economist*, April 2008, pp. 12–13. Reproduced by permission.

likely to hold a credit card. Attitudes toward borrowing have changed as well; for example, people increasingly borrow to finance things like vacations and living expenses.

While credit card usage has increased across the income spectrum, the largest increases occurred among lower-income groups. (See the accompanying table. [not shown]) Among those in the lowest 20 percent of the income distribution, the fraction with credit card debt nearly doubled between 1989 and 2004, and their median credit card debt increased to $1,000 from $400. For those in the next lowest 20 percent, the fraction with credit card debt increased by 51 percent, and their median debt doubled to $1,800.[2]

Data from the Federal Deposit Insurance Corp. (FDIC) provide some perspective as to the magnitude of the credit card industry.[3] Between 1992 and 2006, the total dollar amount of credit card loans nearly tripled while the dollar amount of loans that are 90 days delinquent more than tripled. At the end of 2006, FDIC-insured institutions had $385 billion in credit card loans to individuals, and $6.5 billion were past due 90 days or more (1.7 percent of the total).

Between 1992 and 2006, the total dollar amount of credit card loans nearly tripled while the dollar amount of loans that are 90 days delinquent more than tripled.

What's in the Balance?

In addition to carrying a balance, borrowers do not appear to rush to pay off their credit cards. Several economists have found that some consumers carry credit card balances even though they have sufficient funds in the bank to pay off their high-interest debt. Using data from the 2001 SCF and the 2000–2002 Consumer Expenditure Survey, economist Irina Telyukova categorized households into three groups: borrowers, savers, and borrowers-and-savers. She found that about 28 percent of those surveyed had at least $500 both in credit card debt and liquid assets. This group—the borrowers-and-savers—held an average credit card debt of $5,766 and an average of $7,237 in liquid assets. Furthermore, the average interest rate on the debt was 13.7 percent and only about 1 percent on their liquid assets.

To explain why some continued to hold both high-interest debt and liquid assets, Telyukova hypothesized that households keep liquid assets for payments where cash is required.[4] While many of these expenses are predictable, others may arise in an emergency. To protect themselves in the event such a case arises, households may forgo paying off credit card debt in order to keep cash available.[5]

I Want It All, and I Want It Now

Another increasingly common form of short-term debt is the payday loan. From 2000 to 2003, the industry quadrupled in size to $40 billion.[6] Payday loans are designed to lend small amounts of money for short amounts of time, usually two weeks. Typical interest rates for two weeks can range from 15 to 18 percent, which translates into about a 400 percent annual interest rate. Payments are due on the borrower's payday but may be renewed with additional fees.

Similar to credit cards, payday loans have become popular among lower-income households. A Center for Responsible Lending (CRL) report argues that 90 percent of lenders' revenue comes from borrowers who have five or more loans per year, not one-time borrowers.[7] To demonstrate, an average borrower renews a loan eight times and ends up paying back $793 for a $325 loan. According to the CRL estimates, Americans paid $4.2 billion in payday loan fees in 2005.

Economists Paige Skiba and Jeremy Tobacman found that applicants for payday loans from a particular lender in Texas had an average monthly income of $1,699 and $235 in their checking account.[8] Additionally, 77 percent of the applicants were black or Hispanic and 62 percent were women. Based on the study's results, it seems that access to loans can lead to recidivism. Within one year, a consumer whose first-time application for a payday loan was approved would apply for another loan an average of 8.4 more times; in comparison, a consumer whose first-time application was rejected would apply 1.8 more times on average. The total loans for the former were for $2,200 with roughly $400 in accompanying fees/interest payments.

You Get What You (Don't) Pay For

Americans appear willing to trade substantial interest payments for access to short-term credit markets. But, does this new behavior have detrimental long-term effects? Based on data from the American Bankruptcy Institute, for every 1 million adults in the U.S. population, about 1,800 filed for bankruptcy in 1980, a number that increased to about 7,300 in 2004.[9]

According to a study by economist Michelle White, an increase in the amount of revolving debt per household (especially in the form of credit card debt) coincided with the increase in personal bankruptcy filings from the 1980s to 2005. There were 5.4 times more bankruptcies in 2004 than in 1980, and revolving debt per household was 4.6 times larger in 2004 than in 1980. White discussed other possible explanations for the increase in bankruptcy filings, such as job loss and medical bills. However, these types of adverse events have not increased since 1980. Therefore, she concluded that the rise in personal bankruptcies can be attributed in large part to the rise in credit card debt.

Similarly, the payday loan applicants in Skiba and Tobacman's study were six times more likely to file for bankruptcy between January 2001 and June 2005 than the general population in Texas. The bankruptcy filing rate for the state was 0.38 percent per year versus 2.3 percent per year for loan applicants.

Skiba and Tobacman tested whether access to payday loans increased bankruptcy filings.[10] They found no effect on the number of Chapter 7 filings, but the number of Chapter 13 filings increased significantly.[11] Within one year of his first payday loan, a borrower's likelihood of filing Chapter 13 increased by 1.9 percentage points, and within two years, the likelihood was 2.5 percentage points higher.

As with any kind of loan, credit cards and payday loans can be convenient for some people as a means to borrow money for a relatively short period of time. However, the recent rise in short-term liabilities—especially by lower-income households—may have long-term implications for the economy as demonstrated by their apparent correlation with bankruptcy filings.

Endnotes

1. See Bucks, Kennickell and Moore (2006) and Black and Morgan (1999) for a description of changes in credit-card holders.

2. Note that the numbers are only for families with credit card balances.

3. The data include all institutions insured by the FDIC. See www2.fdic.gov/sdi/sob/.

4. "Cash" here refers to cash and similar payments, e.g., check, debit card.

5. For the average household in each group, the borrower-and-saver kept 3.4 times more, the borrower kept 0.1 times more and the saver kept 10 times more money in the bank than needed for cash-only goods in a typical month.

6. From the Center for Responsible Lending. See www.responsiblelending.org/issues/payday/briefs/page.jsp?itemID=29557924.

7. See www.responsiblelending.org/pdfs/rr012-Financial_
   Quicksand-1106.pdf.

8. The authors obtained data from a provider of financial
   services.

9. New bankruptcy laws effective in October 2005 made it
   harder for consumers to file for Chapter 7 bankruptcy,
   which caused a sharp increase in the bankruptcy rate in
   the first three quarters of 2005 and a sharp decline in
   2006.

10. To obtain a loan, the applicant's credit score must
    reach a certain threshold. Of first-time applicants, 99.6
    percent below that threshold were rejected, and 96.9
    percent above the threshold were accepted. Because the
    difference between a consumer whose application was
    barely accepted and one whose application was barely
    rejected is very small, the authors focused their analysis
    on those near the acceptance threshold.

11. Chapter 7 bankruptcy eliminates all dischargeable
    debts, and Chapter 13 bankruptcy creates a long term
    repayment plan.

References

Black, Sandra E.; and Morgan, Donald P. "Meet the New
Borrowers." Federal Reserve Bank of New York, *Current
Issues in Economics and Finance*, February 1999, Vol. 5, No.
3, pp. 1–6.

Bucks, Brian K.; Kennickell, Arthur B.; and Moore, Kevin
B. "Recent Changes in U.S. Family Finances: Evidence from
the 2001 and 2004 Survey of Consumer Finances." Federal
Reserve Bulletin, March 2006.

King, Uriah; Parrish, Leslie; and Tanik, Ozlem. "Financial
Quicksand: Payday Lending Sinks Borrowers in Debt with

$4.2 Billion in Predatory Fees Every Year." Center for Responsible Lending report, November 2006.

Skiba, Paige Marta; and Tobacman, Jeremy. "Do Payday Loans Cause Bankruptcy?" Unpublished manuscript, Oxford University, November 2007.

Telyukova, Irina A. "Household Need for Liquidity and the Credit Card Debt Puzzle." Unpublished manuscript, University of California, San Diego, December 2007.

White, Michelle J. "Bankruptcy Reform and Credit Cards." *Journal of Economic Perspectives*, Fall 2007, Vol. 21, No. 4, pp. 175–99.

Economic Necessity Drives the Surge in Consumer Debt

Christian E. Weller

Christian E. Weller is a senior fellow at the Center for American Progress, a progressive think tank in Washington, D.C.

The past few years have been marked by a record run-up in consumer debt. Total household debt grew more than four times faster between March 2001 and the middle of 2006 than it did in the 1990s.

This rise in consumer debt occurred against the backdrop of a number of important macro trends. After the previous business cycle ended in March 2001, families saw the weakest employment growth since the Great Depression, stagnant wages, and declining health and pension benefits. At the same time, costs for housing, a college education, health care, and transportation rose sharply. To bridge the growing gap between income and costs, families borrowed heavily, sending consumer debt to record highs.

This debt surge was widely shared across demographic groups. In fact, it was more pronounced among middle-income and white families than among their counterparts. Consumer credit became an equalizer of financial insecurity.

Families Borrow to Make Ends Meet

The data suggest that the run-up in debt is more a consequence of economic necessities than of profligate spending. While the desire for instant gratification is probably a small contributing factor, it is far outweighed by the need of families to borrow more amid sluggish income growth and rising prices. In fact, families have become more willing to be financially responsible over time. Further, it is argued that families borrowed to invest, especially in real estate. The data, though, suggest that families did not see a markedly sharper rise in their wealth in recent years than in previous years when debt growth was more subdued. In addition, much of the wealth gains that families saw were due to a boom in the real estate market, which many economists believe to be overvalued.

The debt boom of the past few years occurred against the back drop of a weak labor market and rapidly rising prices for important consumer items. Real family incomes did not rise in any single year between 2000 and 2004, before recovering a little in 2005, but median family incomes were still below those in 2001. The earnings for men and women who worked full-time all year declined again in 2005, to their lowest level since 1997 for men, and since 2000 for women. Almost all groups saw either declines or flat incomes during this period. From 2000 to 2005, real incomes of black families declined by 8.2%, those of Hispanic families by 4.3%, and of white families by 2.5%. Low-income families' incomes declined by 7.5% compared to a decrease of 3.3% for middle income families.

The data suggest that the run-up in debt is more a consequence of economic necessities than of profligate spending.

Simultaneously, prices rose sharply. Health care costs shot up the fastest, but other costs also grew. Food, housing, and household operations all saw average quarterly price increases of 2–3% between 1990 and 2006. In comparison, expenditures on smaller consumption items grew at about half that rate.

To manage rising prices and stagnant and declining income, families borrowed more. By June 2006, families had amassed debt equivalent to 129.3 percent of disposable income after rising on average 1.3 percentage points per quarter from March 2001 through March 2006. In comparison, from

December 1995 through March 2001 it grew by an average of 0.4 percentage points, four times slower. Simultaneously, the share of disposable income used to pay off debt reached a record high of 14.4% in June 2006.

Household Debt Has Risen
Faster Than Income

Using survey data from the Survey of Consumer Finances (SCF), trends in household debt by demographic characteristics are discernible. The survey data show that all families saw sharp increases in the amount of debt they owed relative to their total income. However, middle income families and white families saw larger increases in their debt to income ratios than for their counterparts.

This pattern of debt growth relative to income shows differing combinations of the need to borrow and access to credit. The comparatively lower growth of debt to income for low income families, for example, couples the need to borrow with limited access to credit. Low income families are disproportionately renters and thus cannot offer their home as collateral. They have also seen less income growth than their counterparts, which raises their need to borrow faster than for other families, but gives them less collateral to borrow against. For high income families, credit access is less limited since home ownership is widespread and income growth has been stronger than elsewhere, but the need to borrow is also less pronounced. In the middle of the income scale, the need to borrow meets credit access. Middle income families have seen comparatively weak income growth, but they also experienced increases in home ownership and in the value of their homes, thus giving them more access to credit. Hence, the recent run-up in household debt is more pronounced in the middle of the income scale.

Debt Payments a Key Consideration

It is not debt levels, but debt payments that often matter more to families. After all, families borrow to invest in their own future, such as college education, to buy a home, or to make ends meet when their income is less than they had expected. In each case, though, families will have to figure out if they can afford the payments on their debt. Lenders, such as banks and credit card companies, take a similar approach, when they ask borrowers to submit pay stubs for a loan application or when they consider applicants' credit reports, which are heavily influenced by borrowers' incomes.

The figures show similar trends for debt to income. In particular, debt payments relative to income rose faster for families in the third and fourth income quintile than for lower or higher income families. As a result, debt payments were highest in 2004 for families in the fourth income quintile with 21%. Families in the middle quintile followed closely with median payments of 20% of their income. Also, debt payments rose faster for whites than for blacks between 2001 and 2004 and faster for whites than for Latinos between 1989 and 2004.

Importantly, the growth in debt payments relative to income shows that the rise in debt levels relative to income was not just a consequence of lower costs of credit. If households only borrowed because it was cheaper, their debt levels should have risen only enough to keep their payments steady in comparison to their incomes. The fact that payments relative to income rose and in some cases reached their highest level ever, despite the lowest interest rates in decades, shows that factors, other than the costs of credit, were at work in determining how much families borrowed in recent years.

Debt as an Investment Tool

In the aggregate, it is items that can be classified as investments in a family's future that are at the heart of the growth in loans, instead of frivolous consumption. As a share of total debt, home related loans grew to their highest level since the Federal Reserve has conducted this survey. According to these data, 81% of all loans outstanding in 2004 were taken out for home purchases and home improvements, up from 79% in 2001. The second most important reason for loans were car loans, but as a share of the total, they declined by one percentage point from 2001 to 2004. All loans for goods and services, which include debt for consumer electronics, but also for medical care, remained steady at 5% of the total. Similarly, education loans stayed at a constant 3% of the total. That is, at the aggregate level the big driver of consumer debt are housing related loans, while loans for consumption items, such as cars or goods and services, are declining or stable as a share of the total amount of outstanding debt.

The big driver of consumer debt are housing related loans, while loans for consumption items, such as cars or goods and services, are declining or stable as a share of the total amount of outstanding debt.

When considering changes of loans taken out for each purpose, it becomes even clearer that loans for investments were a more important driver of debt growth than loans for consumption items. In inflation adjusted terms, the median amount of home related loans for families that had such loans rose by 26%, as fast as education related loans. In comparison, the median amount of car loans grew by only 11% and the median amount of loans for goods and services increased by only 21% between 2001 and 2004. Moreover, by 2004, the median amount of education loans was three times as large as the median amount of loans for goods and services.

Another way to look at the data is to consider loans taken out for specific purposes relative to family income. Again, the largest increases are noticeable for home and education loans. Also, the relative size difference between education loans and loans for goods and services stays as loans for the former are about three times as large as loans for the latter relative to income. Hence, the data show a debt boom that is predominantly driven by families investing in their future.

Debt-Financed Investments Do Not Create Wealth

Although families generally do not take on loans to finance investments that they sell quickly, it is occasionally argued that the debt boom of the past few years has allowed families to invest in more assets than otherwise would have been the case. If this is the case, we should have also seen faster wealth growth than in the past. Considering total family wealth trends, there is no clear indication that the accelerated debt growth after 2000 was widely associated with equally large wealth increases.

Take, for instance, total accessible wealth relative to income. Total accessible wealth is the sum of financial assets, including retirement savings accounts, plus real estate assets minus all debt. Relative to income it rose for the median family to 260% in 2004 from 245% in 2001. This shows an accelerated increase in the ratio of accessible wealth to income after 2000, when debt growth also accelerated. However, this link between more debt and more wealth only shows up when housing wealth is included in the calculation. When only financial wealth is included, the financial wealth to income ratio declined for the population as a whole from 2001 to 2004. Insofar as financial wealth is a measure of financial security for families who cannot or do not always want to sell their homes to pay for other necessities, the recent debt boom meant a reduction in financial security for America's middle class.

One may imagine that families willingly traded off financial security if they could increase home ownership and home equity instead, although this would contradict basic financial economic rules of wealth diversification. Home ownership rates did indeed increase from 2001 to 2004, but not at an accelerated rate. The rate of growth in homeownership from 2001 to 2004 was the same as from 1998 to 2001. Moreover, the accelerated housing wealth was due in large part to an extraordinary run-up in home prices, which many economists believed to be overvalued.

The figures show that America's families built up housing wealth at the expense of financial wealth, during a time of accelerated indebtedness. In some cases, the two trends may have been related—more debt allowed families to purchase more valuable homes—but the data do not necessarily support a broad connection between the two. Moreover, even if there was a link between families' indebtedness and housing wealth, it seems important to keep in mind that not all housing wealth created after 2000 will necessarily be sustained. After all, many observers considered the housing market after 2000 overvalued, i.e., much of the rise in home equity relative to income could disappear as the housing bubble deflates.

Considering trends in families' wealth, it is clear that there is no clear link between more debt and more wealth, as one would expect if the debt boom was caused by families wanting to build more wealth. Instead, where debt growth created more wealth, it did so only with respect to housing wealth. As a result more household wealth was tied up in the families' home, which made it more vulnerable than before to a decline in home values. Specifically, a larger portion of families' assets were tied up in real estate and families owned a smaller share of their own homes than before. This means that as the housing market deflates; household wealth and home equity should decline more than would be the case with less relative investment in real estate and less real estate debt.

Rising Debt Does Not Necessarily Inhibit Saving

There is additional evidence that debt growth had more to do with lack of income growth and borrowing for ever more costly consumption items than with a lack of self-control. Specifically, survey questions that address self-described saving behavior, and are correlated with wealth creation, show that families have become more inclined to save over time. Since 1989, the SCF has included the following question on saving behavior:

Which of the following statements comes closest to describing your saving habits?

- Don't save—usually spend more than income

- Don't save—usually spend about as much as income

- Save whatever is left over at the end of the month—no regular plan

- Save income of one family member, spend the other

- Spend regular income, save other income

- Save regularly by putting money aside each month

For simplicity reasons, respondents are divided into "savers" and "non-savers." Non-savers are those who answered yes to self-identify with any of the first three answers, while savers are defined as those respondents who self-identified with the last three answers. Specifically, the value "1" is given to non-savers and the value "2" to savers.

The figures show a few trends. First, savings attitudes have improved. The attitude toward savings rose by 5% percent from 1989 to 2004. Also, from 2001 to 2004, there was no change in savings attitude. The data do not support the notion that the United States experienced eroding self-control, which would explain the accelerated indebtedness after 2000. Moreover, the indebtedness among "saver" families has grown at about the same rate as for "non-saver" families. The debt to income ratio grew from 74% in 2001 to 103% in 2004 for "savers", while it rose from 82% to 109% for "non-saver" families. As people become more willing to save and as debt levels rise at about the same rate regardless of saving attitude, there is no evidence that the recent accelerated debt growth can be attributed to declining personal responsibility.

As people become more willing to save and as debt levels rise at about the same rate regardless of saving attitude, there is no evidence that the recent accelerated debt growth can be attributed to declining personal responsibility.

Vulnerability Is Tied to Housing, Not Debt Level

Against the backdrop of a weak labor market and much higher prices, many families expanded their debt. This rise in debt is more likely a result of economic necessity than of profligate spending. Much of the new debt was used to pay for necessary investment items, such as homes and education, and not consumption items. But, the debt and housing booms left families financially more vulnerable. Much of the improvements in wealth were due to an inflated housing market, which meant that families became more exposed with their total assets to a possibly deflating housing market. And, because of the commensurate debt boom, families' home equity was also particularly exposed to a decline in home values. This increased vulnerability indicates that the debt boom was likely not a deliberate investment decision to boost household wealth, but rather a consequence of accelerated housing appreciation that left families financially more vulnerable. In addition, survey evidence indicates that families became more reluctant to borrow for consumption than in the past.

Increased Debt Levels Threaten Middle-Class Lifestyles

John Gallagher

John Gallagher is a business writer for the Detroit Free Press.

What does bankrupt Detroit-area auto mechanic Ernie Berthet have in common with Wall Street?

Both have been humbled by bad debt, the thread that ties the economic struggles of ordinary Americans to the once-venerable financial houses brought to their knees in recent weeks [in 2008].

It was Berthet's mortgage foreclosure, multiplied by at least a million other bad home loans across the country, that rocked America's financial system and moved the nation toward the biggest business rescue plan in history.

The numbers on Wall Street are dizzyingly large. But brought down to the level of just one distressed borrower, the story shows how even modest levels of debt, if made unmanageable by a layoff, divorce, illness or other hardship, can turn tragic.

Economic Hardship Can Lead to Bankruptcy

Like a lot of bankruptcy filers, Berthet, a 51-year-old Dearborn Heights [Michigan] resident, saw his problems mount not from a profligate lifestyle but from simple misfortune linked with perhaps too-easy credit.

His modest, one-story house in a working-class area cost $82,000. He had a zero-down, adjustable-rate mortgage that reset from 7.35% to 10.35% and then to 13.35%. Losing his job and owing child-care payments to his former wife put him in the red.

"I'm a mechanic by trade," he says. "I was a contract worker, worked in a couple different dealerships. It seems like I'd just get caught up, got all kinds of overtime, and then—boom!—we got laid off," he says.

Unable to pay his bills, Berthet filed for bankruptcy and gave up his house in foreclosure this summer.

"The way the state of the economy was, when I bought my home, I planned on living in my home until I died, but the times they are a-changin'," Berthet says.

If Wall Street's problems are getting most of the headlines now, debt problems for most of this decade have been posing a large and growing challenge to maintaining a traditional middle-class standard of living for ordinary Americans.

Debt Subsidizes the American Dream

The problems on Wall Street and those facing Main Street thus are twisted together in a pervasive tangle. If Wall Street's problems are getting most of the headlines now, debt problems for most of this decade have been posing a large and growing challenge to maintaining a traditional middle-class standard of living for ordinary Americans.

Today, debt pervades all aspects of American life:

- The average household now holds more than $110,000 in mortgage and other debt, against annual personal savings of around $400, according to figures from the Federal Reserve Board and other government bodies that track the economy.

- American consumers today collectively owe $2.5 trillion on their credit cards and in car payments and similar loans. That's up 150% from 1994, an increase more than four times greater than inflation over the same time.

- New college graduates carry more student-loan debt than ever. The nonprofit Project on Student Debt reports that by the time they graduate, nearly two-thirds of students at four-year colleges and universities have student loan debt, compared with less than one-half of graduating students in 1993. Over the past decade, debt levels for graduating seniors with student loans more than doubled from $9,250 to $19,200—a 108% increase, or 58% after accounting for inflation—the project reports.

Borrowers Have Taken On Too Much Debt

Scott Howland, a 2003 graduate of the University of Michigan, has a common debt story at age 28. A ticket office manager for Palace Sports & Entertainment, Howland graduated with $22,000 in student loan debt, has a $150,000 mortgage on his house in Madison Heights [Michigan] and owes $5,000 on credit cards.

He's getting married soon and plans to help pay his fiancée's credit-card balance of around $15,000.

He says his student loans require a minimum monthly payment of $138, which he has automatically withdrawn from his savings.

"For a while there I was trying to pay a little bit more every month, get more on the principal, trying to almost pay double sometimes, but then other expenses crept up and it got to the point where I can only pay the minimum on this and I need to focus my money on the other debts," he says.

The nation's debt burden has soared since the late 1990s, much of it tied to the bubble in housing prices between 2000 and 2005. Americans added about $1 trillion in new mortgage debt—including home equity debt—per year since 2000, and many families borrowed still more on credit cards.

When home prices collapsed, much of that new accumulated debt could no longer be supported and homes couldn't be sold, at least for what was owed on them. But by then, Americans owed more than they made. Since 2002, debt has exceeded disposable income in America by an ever-growing margin. In 1990, debt equaled 78% of disposable income; as of 2007, the figure was 129%.

Carrying Too Much Debt Discourages Saving

Types of credit unknown 20 years ago, such as home-equity loans and borrowing against 401(k) retirement accounts, have sapped long-term savings.

Home equity loans became a popular way to borrow against the value of a home in the mid-'90s, and since 1998, such debt in the United States has soared from about $300 billion to more than $1.1 trillion.

Since early 2007, homeowners owe more on their houses than they hold in equity. Americans now hold as equity 46.2% of their home values. That's down from 57% in 2001, and represents the first time since World War II that equity levels have shrunk so low.

Stephen J. Church, an investment consultant who heads Piscataqua Research Inc. in Portsmouth, New Hampshire, says some retrenchment in the way Americans live is inevitable. Before 1990, he says, Americans spent about 80% of their incomes on goods and services, paid debt with about 10%, and used the rest for savings or discretionary spending. By 2006, Americans were spending nearly 90% on consumption and 13% to cover debt, meaning they had to borrow just to maintain their lifestyle.

"Basically, we had a strong economy built on a mirage of borrowing. It is right there in the numbers," Church says.

As a result, more and more Americans are facing a significantly bigger burden each month trying to pay down mortgages, credit cards and other types of debt. The U.S. Census Bureau reported last month that 37.5% of American households now spend more than the traditionally safe 30% of income on housing.

By 2006, Americans were spending nearly 90% on consumption and 13% to cover debt, meaning they had to borrow just to maintain their lifestyle.

The Debt Burden Threatens Middle-Class Lifestyles

American living standards, which through the country's history have promised an ever-improving way of life for each new generation, already were under threat as middle-class incomes stagnated. Adjusted for inflation, middle-class households earn about $400 less today than they did in 1999, the Census Bureau reports.

Now the borrowing spree of the past decade threatens to make that problem a lot worse. With personal consumption accounting for 70% of the U.S. economy, any cutting back to pay down this mountain of debt threatens a slowdown for the economy—and a further lowering of standards of living for millions of Americans.

Middle-Class Families Need to Reduce Spending

Ann Howard, a bankruptcy attorney from Southfield [Michigan], says the lesson of recent financial woes is simple: The party's over.

"I think it's been a real wake-up call for everybody because you just can't assume that you're always going to make what you're making now or what you made two years ago," Howard says. "You have to keep your expenses low enough so you can ride through the storm if there is one."

Responsible debt, of course, will remain an integral part of financial life in America, with borrowed money paying for everything from cars and homes to complex corporate deals.

"I don't want to create the wrong impression that all debt is bad debt," says economist Jared Bernstein of the Washington, D.C.-based think tank Economic Policy Institute, noting that many families borrow for college education and other productive uses. But he adds that many struggling families borrowed not for long-term goals but simply to keep up, especially as paychecks lost ground to inflation.

"In many ways, lots of middle-income families compensated for their lack of good, old-fashioned income growth by taking on more debt," Bernstein says.

With Americans borrowing and spending so freely, they were saving less than ever, government data show. Personal savings as a percentage of disposable income has dwindled to less than 1% today from nearly 8% in the early 1990s.

With incomes stagnating and using debt to keep up, many Americans placed themselves in a position where any unexpected setback could send household finances into a tailspin.

"We all know that the expenses that really hurt you financially aren't necessarily the predictable ones," Howard says. "Obviously gas and food have gone crazy, but you have the transmission that goes or the $1,200 deductible on your health insurance when your kid has an appendix rupture."

Credit Card Debt Is a Major Culprit

Veronica Smith, a debt counselor with the nonprofit Green-Path Debt Solutions office in Roseville [Michigan], says it's common for people who come to her office to have credit card debt equal to a year's salary at a job they lost.

Howard agrees. "It's a very predictable pattern," she says. "You're going along and then somebody loses a job or somebody has surgery or someone loses their overtime, but you still have all your typical expenses that your income went to. So what do you do? You prop up your household with credit cards and you do that as long as you can."

Howard adds that debt-fueled problems are moving up the income chain.

"I'm seeing a different kind of client now than I've seen before. It's hitting the upper middle class," she says. One client, a real estate professional, saw his annual earnings drop from more than $200,000 a couple of years ago to less than $15,000 today, Howard says.

The consumer advocacy Web site *www.cardratings.com* reports that there are now more than 600 million credit cards in circulation, with the average American carrying four cards. About 60% of cardholders carry over a balance from month to month, often totaling in the thousands of dollars.

This debt has helped generate billions of dollars in profits for the credit-card industry, and every dollar of that ultimately came out of consumers' pockets.

The psychic toll on Americans who see their lives disrupted by excess debt can be enormous, Howard says.

"They're overwhelmed, they're completely stressed out, they're depressed, they're tired," she says of clients who come to her office.

Excessive Debt Prevents People from Saving for Retirement

Lynn O'Shaughnessy

Lynn O'Shaughnessy writes about financial issues for USA Today.

At age 30, Bryan Short has, by any standard, achieved professional success since graduating from Boston College and law school at the College of William and Mary. Yet despite his job as a Washington mergers-and-acquisitions lawyer, he's nowhere near as financially secure as he expected to be by now.

He and his wife own one car and rent a 500-square-foot studio apartment. More than one-third of his take-home pay is gobbled up by repayment of college and law-school debt. Children are unaffordable right now. And retirement savings? They've barely begun.

"Despite being what most would consider clearly upper-middle class, highly educated and almost assuredly on no one's pity party list, I can assure you we live an extremely modest life," says Short, whose wife, Regina, is pursuing an MBA at Johns Hopkins University.

Employee Pensions Are a Thing of the Past

For years, experts have warned that too many of the USA's 79 million baby boomers aren't financially ready for their coming retirements. Yet, if the boomers have had it hard, it's nothing compared with those next in line: Generation X—people such as the Shorts. The Gen Xers, generally defined as those born from 1965 through 1980—now 27 to 43 years old—have even less assurance than the boomers of receiving company pensions and projected Social Security benefits.

In 1979, when the oldest Gen Xers were teenagers, the sole retirement plan for 62% of workers was a traditional pension, according to the Employee Benefit Research Institute (EBRI). By 2005, when most of the Gen Xers had joined the workforce, that number had flipped: 63% of employees found themselves covered only by voluntary 401(k) plans. So much for the corporate safety net.

On top of that, the Gen Xers' life expectancies, and thus their retirements, will likely exceed even the boomers'. They'll need to save more aggressively. Yet, burdened by high housing costs, stifling college debt, stagnating wages, and outsize health insurance and gas prices, Gen Xers are saving too little for retirement, just as workplace benefits have shrunk.

According to the EBRI, more than one in three workers ages 35 to 44 aren't setting aside any money for retirement. Among those ages 25 to 34, 45% aren't saving.

Burdened by high housing costs, stifling college debt, stagnating wages, and outsize health insurance and gas prices, Gen Xers are saving too little for retirement, just as workplace benefits have shrunk.

Generation X Faces an Unsustainable Standard of Living

The Center for Retirement Research at Boston College has calculated that 48% of Gen Xers are at risk of being unable to maintain their standard of living in retirement, says Andrew Eschtruth, the center's communication's director. Compared with the boomers, Eschtruth adds, the Gen Xers "always have the highest at-risk scores. The changing retirement landscape is gradually becoming more challenging."

"One of the biggest issues facing the Gen Xers," observes Pam Hess, director of retirement research at Hewitt Associates and a Gen Xer herself, "is lots of competing priorities, juggling lots of different costs and financial priorities. It will continue to be a struggle."

Consumer debt is one of the main reasons. Nine out of 10 consumers in their 30s are in debt, compared with 76% of those in their 20s, according to the Federal Reserve's Survey of Consumer Finances. In a recent Charles Schwab study of more than 2,000 Gen Xers nationwide, 45% of respondents said they had too much debt to think about saving.

Gen Xers also are the first generation to graduate from college with significant student loan debt. About 20% of adults in their 30s are still paying college loans, according to the Federal Reserve study; the median balance exceeds $13,000. Yet, even as Gen Xers continue to grapple with college debt, experts tell them they need to be putting aside money for retirement, as well as for college savings for their children.

"This generation is in the ironic position of paying for their own student loans and feeling the pressure to put away for their own kids for college," says Tamara Draut, a Gen Xer herself, a new mom and author of *Strapped: Why America's 20- and 30-Somethings Can't Get Ahead*.

Stagnant Wages Reduce the Earning Power of Generation Xers

Gen Xers also face this harsh reality: The standard of living that most of them have so far managed to achieve falls short of their own parents' standard at the same age. The median income for men now in their 30s, when adjusted for inflation, is 12% lower than what their dads earned three decades earlier, a report by the Economic Mobility Project, an initiative of The Pew Charitable Trusts, concluded.

The mobility project found that from 1974, when many Gen Xers were children, until 2004, when most were in the workforce, family income rose only 9%. And most of that gain came from 1964 to 1994—before the Gen Xers even started thinking about résumés.

Why did income decline just as Gen Xers began their careers? A key reason is that pay had risen so steadily while many of them were children—thanks to women entering the workforce in greater numbers—that pressure for wage growth had declined by the time the Gen Xers began working.

"Now that women's workforce participation has stabilized, where will the next bump in family income come from?" asks John Morton, director of the Economic Mobility Project. "With rapidly rising costs at a time of stagnating income, the question is, 'What do you have left?'"

Costs Have Increased on Essential Goods

Gen Xers also had the unfortunate timing of becoming adults in a period when the share of income that Americans spend on what most people see as essential needs, such as a home, health insurance, and cars, has soared. Elizabeth Warren, a Harvard law professor and expert on middle-class finances, has concluded that the soaring inflation-adjusted price of such necessities has negated the extra spending power that female workers provided.

Relying on government figures, Warren found that health insurance soared 74%, in inflation-adjusted dollars, since 1970 and that the mortgage payment that a median-income family is paying for a three-bedroom, one-bath house jumped 76%.

On an inflation-adjusted basis, the average cost of owning a car has declined from a generation ago. But auto-related expenses jumped 52% because the typical family now owns at least two vehicles.

Gen Xers don't need experts to tell them what they already know. Their optimism is already flagging. The 2007 Retirement Confidence Survey by the EBRI found that just 28% of workers between ages 35 and 44 were "very confident" of having enough money to retire comfortably. In the 2008 survey, even fewer—16%—felt so sanguine.

Lori Brown, 40, a hairdresser in DeKalb, Illinois, who's married to a sheet-metal worker, is one of millions of Gen Xers who have struggled to raise their living standard without the means to do so. The Browns, who earn around $75,000 a year, have talked repeatedly through the years about buying a home. Yet, they've never managed to do it.

The couple pay a fairly modest $645 a month to rent one floor of a house. But taking on a mortgage seems too risky, especially when Lori depends on commissions, and her husband's work is seasonal. Lori says her clients needle her about it.

"Some of them," she says, "hound me about why we don't have a home, and we're throwing money down the drain and making the landlord rich."

The Government Encourages Saving for Retirement

With so many Gen Xers struggling to set aside money for retirement, Congress has tried to make the savings habit routine. Landmark legislation—the Pension Protection Act of 2006—is turning more Gen Xers, along with other Americans, into savers. One way the law is beginning to achieve that goal is by encouraging employers to automatically enroll new workers in 401(k) plans.

Just as important, the pension act paved the way for more businesses to set a default 401(k) investment option for participants that delivers more octane in the long run than an ultra-safe money market. Hewitt Associates found that money funds were the default option for 68% of 401(k) plans in 2001, compared with 17% in 2007.

Employers are embracing target-retirement mutual funds, which contain a mix of stock and bond funds that turns more conservative as a participant nears a target retirement year. Today, 78% of surveyed companies use such funds for their default investment.

Many Generation Xers Do Not Understand Investment Options

If you look at Gen X-related research conducted by Charles Schwab, it's easy to appreciate why making the act of investing as simple as possible is necessary.

Robert O'Neill, a senior vice president at Charles Schwab who oversees the firm's Gen X initiative, said Schwab found that Gen Xers often don't understand investment basics. Many, for instance, don't realize that an investor can contribute to both a 401(k) plan and an IRA. This might help explain why 82% of Gen Xers have no IRA, according to a Schwab survey.

For now, most Gen Xers ... are receiving their investment advice from the very people who used to nag them to clean their room and take out the garbage: their parents.

Schwab also found that many Gen Xers are more comfortable initially investing beyond their workplace retirement plan through checking and savings accounts. Consequently, Schwab launched a high-yield checking account aimed at Gen Xers, and a website (*www.schwabmoneyandmore.com*) tailored for them.

For now, most Gen Xers, according to Schwab, are receiving their investment advice from the very people who used to nag them to clean their room and take out the garbage: their parents.

Generation Xers Are Skeptical About the Future

Some Gen Xers say they hold fewer illusions than previous generations did about the stability of whatever job they hold—or might hold in the future.

Skepticism about job stability, for example, led Melissa Garland, 37, who works as a multimedia developer in Baltimore, to become a part-time entrepreneur. She launched a ghost-tour-guide business in Baltimore that she says is flourishing.

"Companies have no loyalty, which is why I wanted to start my own business," she says. "Anybody could be out on the street at any time."

Some specialists suggest that Gen Xers, faced with escalating financial obligations and shakier job situations, have developed a wary, skeptical stance toward the corporate world.

"They want to make the most of their opportunities," says Rebecca Schreiber, a financial planner in Silver Spring, Maryland, who specializes in counseling Gen X clients. "They've got the dot-com boom and Enron behind them, which makes them skeptical about relying on any corporation entities.

"The previous generation is panicked about retirement, and this fear has wormed its way into the hearts of Gen X," she says. "Gen Xers are constantly reminded of the mounting cost to retire."

Schreiber says she remains optimistic about Generation X. "They just need a little education," she says hopefully.

Low-Income Consumers Are Unable to Pay Off High-Interest Debt

Tamara Draut

Tamara Draut is the director of the Economic Opportunity Program at Dēmos, a non-partisan public policy research and advocacy organization. She also is the author of Strapped: Why America's 20- and 30-Somethings Can't Get Ahead.

Victor and Eloise represent the new face of debt in America. Together, they've worked in a series of low-wage jobs that include stints at fast-food restaurants, small factories, and hotels. Technically, they are not poor according to the government's official definition of "poverty," but the economic vulnerability of the working poor and the near-poor are increasingly similar. The couple, whom I interviewed for my recent book, live in Montgomery, Alabama, with their two children, aged 4 and 14. They own their own home, which they bought in 2000 after their second child was born.

Today, after more than a decade of working low-wage jobs, the couple's annual income has risen to about $50,000, more than double the poverty-line for a family of four. But their long years of subsistence living have left them with high-interest debt totaling $13,000. They're paying a 25 percent annual percentage rate on a $3,000 credit-card balance that paid for new tires and alignment work on their car, as well as for a new stove for their kitchen. They also have three personal installment loans totaling more than $9,000, all at interest rates of 25 percent or higher. These loans were used to help cover bills while Eloise was on maternity leave, to help pay for a used car, and to help repair the family's home air conditioner. After years of barely making a dent in the principal, the couple now pays $345 a month to a credit company that negotiated lower rates and makes payments on their behalf toward one of their credit cards and on two of their installment loans, but they still pay over $500 month, mostly in interest, in past loans that financed basic living expenses.

Victor and Eloise symbolize what many in the financial industry enthusiastically champion as the democratization of credit. Its cheerleaders remind us that two decades ago, virtually all lenders—save, perhaps, for the local pawnbroker or loan shark—would have snubbed Victor and Eloise. But today, thanks to technological change and deregulation, the low-income market is a bonanza for lenders.

Thanks to technological change and deregulation, the low-income market is a bonanza for lenders.

With ever-more-sophisticated underwriting technology, lenders say they can better calculate risk and price loans accordingly. In addition, deregulation in the early 1980s and '90s all but eliminated interest rates and fee limits. The result is a tidal wave of high-cost credit targeted to low-income individuals, particularly in communities of color, at interest rates once considered usurious but now regarded as perfectly legitimate. It's a great system for everyone but the borrower.

The unleashing of exorbitantly priced credit coincided with two other important trends: the steady decline in earnings power of low-income households and the shredding of our public safety net. As already strapped low-income households found themselves falling further behind, they also found their mailboxes stuffed with rescue offers of easy and fast credit. And in low-income neighborhoods, storefronts selling fast and expensive loans are now as plentiful as McDonalds selling fast and cheap food.

Consider the payday loan. A borrower simply writes a postdated check and exchanges it for cash from the lender for a fee—typically starting around $15 for each $100 borrowed, or about 300 percent to 440 percent APR [annual percentage rate]. The premise is that in two weeks or so, the lender will cash the check, paying off the loan. However, most borrowers end up extending their loan because they don't have enough funds to cover the postdated check. In fact, according to the Center for Responsible Lending, the average payday loan is renewed eight times, costing the borrower about $800 for an initial loan of $325. The center estimates that $4.2 billion is extracted in payday-loan fees from borrowers' pockets each year.

Low-income households turn to payday loans for many of the same reasons they incur credit-card debt: unexpected expenses or drops in income. Today, about one in three low- to middle-income households have credit-card debt, with an average balance of $6,500 for those with incomes below $35,000. Most of these households aren't indebted because they have a spending problem; they're indebted because they have an income problem. According to a study conducted by Dēmos and the Center for Responsible Lending, 44 percent of low-income indebted households reported that a layoff contributed to their credit-card debt; 20 percent cited medical expenses; 50 percent cited car repairs; and 38 percent cited home repairs.

As all of us can attest, things happen that can cause a financial crunch. For low-income families, however, the likelihood of such things happening is much higher, while emergency reserves are much lower. The ability of these households to save has diminished as incomes at the bottom of the wage distribution have fallen while costs for housing and health care have soared. In addition, our social safety net no longer really catches those who experience a fall: Fewer workers qualify for unemployment insurance, and wage-replacement levels have diminished. The health-care safety net in the form of Medicaid catches the most vulnerable, but it leaves many low-income individuals completely unprotected. And so, unleashed by deregulation that lifted interest-rate caps and limits on fees, major banks have underwritten and financed billions of dollars in loans and extracted billions in high interest rates and fees from low-income families with nowhere else to turn.

Major banks have underwritten and financed billions of dollars in loans and extracted billions in high interest rates and fees from low-income families with nowhere else to turn.

Borrowers need to share responsibility for their indebtedness, but government, like the lending industry, is far from innocent. Over the last three decades, policy-makers have steadily abandoned Americans in and near poverty.

Belatedly, however, the practices of the lending industry are coming under scrutiny. Since January 2007, with the meltdown in sub-prime mortgage loans and the change in Congress, the Senate and House have held multiple hearings on lending-industry practices. Chris Dodd, who chairs the Senate Banking Committee, has signaled that legislation addressing the credit-card industry may be on the way. Meanwhile, an impressive and diverse group of organizations have joined together to form Americans for Fairness in Lending (www.affil.org), whose goal is to raise awareness of abusive lending practices and to call for reregulation.

Restoring responsibility to the lending industry is just one aspect of the remedy, however. The deeper cure for debt as a safety net is to increase earnings and social benefits for the working poor, so that low-income families have the opportunity to move beyond mere subsistence living. That means raising the minimum wage, tearing down barriers to union organizing, providing universal health care, and creating more incentives in the tax code to help these families save and build wealth. Debt is not a safety net, but unless change is forthcoming, it will likely remain the only net available.

Responsible Consumer Credit Increases One's Quality of Life and Fuels the Economy

Matthew Ruben

Matthew Ruben is a supervising editor of PAIS International, a ProQuest database that contains links to journal articles, books, government documents, statistical directories, grey literature, research reports, conference reports, publications of international agencies, microfiche, and Internet material.

Individual consumers have clear incentives not to be saddled with too much debt. Excessive use of credit can result in an arduous repayment process or bankruptcy. Certain cultures view personal debt as immoral. We tend to see less consumer borrowing in Islamic and Asian countries where cultural biases exist against people saddled with debt.

But is debt intrinsically bad for consumers? Access to credit has long been seen as an important part in ensuring a better quality of life, particularly in the United States. Home loans and similar loans were designed to allow families to buy homes and cars with only a job and a modest down payment. And smaller loans (including credit cards) can be used by consumers as a safety net in case of medical emergency or sudden unemployment. Legitimate forms of credit at reasonable rates are essential to the achievement of the proverbial American dream.

Consumer Credit Is Good for the Economy

From a macroeconomic standpoint, consumer credit in the form of low interest rates can help fuel an economy. Since the New Deal [the economic and social reform program enacted by President Franklin D. Roosevelt], Keynesian economics [economic theory espoused by John Maynard Keynes] has promoted greater consumer access to credit, especially during periods of economic decline, in order to increase demand for goods. In other words, when credit is made more available, resulting increases in demands for consumer goods cause an increase in economic production. Consumer spending is the engine of the American economy, and an increase in household debt can be a net benefit for business conditions. In these respects, some level of consumer debt is a healthy and essential ingredient for a modern capitalist economy.

Furthermore, an extensive investigation of historical trends in U.S. consumer behavior finds that as consumer debt has grown since the Great Depression, it has done so in large part because of efforts to promote lending as well as to democratize the lending market. If debt is rising, it's doing so because credit opportunities are expanding. New Deal legislation facilitated the greater availability of guaranteed loans for mortgages, home improvements and cars. The innovations of store credit and credit cards in the 1960s and 1970s further improved access to credit. And, while women and minority groups had been excluded from credit in the post-World War II period, public policy efforts in the 1960s and 1970s provided access to these groups.

Therefore, both a sensibility about debt and an understanding of historical trends in this country would justify a steadily climbing rate of consumer debt in the latter half of the 20th century. Some amount of debt is justifiable. But at what point is there *too much* debt?

Good Debt Turns Bad When It Becomes Unmanageable

From the standpoint of the individual consumer, "too much" is when debt becomes unmanageable and unpayable. Based on statistics from the Federal Reserve Board, disposable income used to make monthly debt payments hovered between 10 and 12 percent between 1980 and 2000, but, following a period of low interest rates, climbed to more than 14 percent by 2006. But does this suggest households are necessarily having a more difficult time servicing their debt?

From the standpoint of the greater economy, "too much" is when debt is high enough that low interest rates aren't adequate to induce further consumption, or when consumers are saddled with too much debt to invest. Furthermore, when delinquencies and bankruptcies become rampant, as was the case in 2008, banks, other lenders, and markets suffer.

Finally, some forms of debt are unhealthy no matter the level of borrowing. Any predatory lending or usury is undesirable, from the standpoint of both the borrower as well as the economy as a whole.

From the standpoint of the borrower, there is always a cost to borrowing, and all debt is taken on because of a desired or needed benefit in return.

Benefits of Debt Depend on Consumers' Circumstances

From the standpoint of the borrower, there is always a cost to borrowing, and all debt is taken on because of a desired or needed benefit in return. But not all debt is the same. . . . [C]onsumer debt can vary greatly in terms of what sort of benefit it can provide and what kinds of risks or costs it entails, particularly among the more common forms of debt.

Mortgages and other secured debt. A secured loan is a loan for which the lender receives collateral in return. Mortgages and car loans are among the most common secured loans. In these cases, collateral is provided to the lending institution in the form of a lien on the title to the property until the loan is paid off in full, and if the borrower defaults on the loan, the lender retains the legal right to repossess the property.

Traditionally (though not always), these types of loans—and mortgages in particular—are offered at a lower interest rates because banks and other lending institutions are taking on less risk, thanks to the provided collateral.

Another factor that makes these loans somewhat more desirable is in the real long-term benefit provided to the borrower. The property provided as a result of the loan is a tangible asset that often provides an economic benefit, such as a place to live or a car to drive. (Although while cars tend to rapidly depreciate, houses tend to retain their economic value.) Of course, a loan taken out to purchase goods which don't provide the same sort of economic benefit in the long run—such as an entertainment system—can also be a secured loan. But many secured loans can be justified by their potentially significant long-term economic benefit to the borrower, and this is no doubt one reason why mortgages are traditionally viewed differently than other forms of consumer debt.

Student loans. Student loans differ from mortgages in that they are usually unsecured loans, meaning that collateral is not provided by the borrower against the provided assets. But because education is associated with higher future incomes, lenders view these loans as less risky than loans of other types, and consumers perceive them as rewarding. Young people who otherwise wouldn't be able to afford higher education gain substantial benefits from student loans in the form of better financial opportunities after earning their degree. So student loan debt is "good" because the borrower is purchasing future earning capability and investing in him- or herself.

In a different sense, student loans are comparable to mortgages in providing an investment in the future. Most workers expect their peak earnings to come later in life. Anticipating higher earnings in future years, consumers can afford to borrow to finance earlier in life and later pay down their debt.

Loans That Carry Higher Interest Rates

Credit cards. Credit cards are another form of unsecured loan, typically offering higher interest rates than long-term secured loans. Other forms of personal loans exist, but because of the relative ease of owning and using a credit card in modern society, credit card debt has grown dramatically. Credit card borrowing is generally considered undesirable because of its association with high interest rates, especially as debt becomes long-term, and its significance is a consequence of the relative convenience of using a credit card. Interest rates can vary dramatically, depending on the state of the economy or the borrower's credit history, but for the most part, interest rates are higher on credit cards than on other forms of personal debt.

Furthermore, even if we consider that many people use credit cards for basic necessities such as utility bills, food, and shelter, the long term benefit of consumables does not typically match the economic benefit of a mortgage or a student loan.

Payday loans. A payday loan is a small, short-term loan provided to a borrower until his or her next payday. Finance charges on payday loans are as a rule very high, and payday loans are often subject to high fees and penalties, varying somewhat depending on local laws. One big advantage of a payday loan is that it doesn't require a credit check, so people with poor credit can borrow money; all that is required is proof of employment and a checking account. Another advantage is in their relative convenience. Today there are more payday loan and check cashing stores in the U.S. than there are McDonald's, Burger King, Sears, J.C. Penney, and Target stores combined. But fees are translated into an estimated 400 to 1000 percent annual interest. While most payday loans are designed to be short-term, many roll over into a period longer than a few weeks, resulting in exorbitantly high rates of interest. For these types of loans, lenders take on a moderate amount of risk by avoiding a credit check, but loans are backed by postdated personal checks and employment verification.

Today there are more payday loan and check cashing stores in the U.S. than there are McDonald's, Burger King, Sears, J.C. Penney, and Target stores combined.

Debt Is Only Bad When It Is Used Irresponsibly

There is obviously a great chasm separating a medical student paying off loans that financed her education and a minimum wage earner paying off a credit card bill that was used to buy Christmas gifts. But each is still a form of consumer debt. Moreover, while one form of debt might appear to be more morally justified from the standpoint of either consumer welfare or the general economy, the cost and benefit of any loan depends on the details. This means that a loan is only as good or as bad as its rate of payment and possible associated fees. These fees can, in turn, be high even with collateral, or low even without it.

Therefore, it would be foolhardy to dismiss credit card debt as bad for the consumer or student loans as a necessarily good investment. Student loans can be usurious. Credit card interest rates can be reasonable (and credit cards can be paid back quickly, before any interest is charged). Even home equity loans can be spent by the borrower for just about whatever he or she wishes (including paying off credit card debt). Another way of putting it would be that consumers who take on debt must be careful only to accept debt they can afford to repay.

Additionally, it makes little sense to think of these debts as being distinct, given that when consumers need to borrow, they likely choose among these options. If a consumer can't access a home equity loan or a student loan, there is a better chance he or she might borrow from a credit card. And if credit cards are not a readily available option, a consumer might resort to a payday loan.

For better or worse, Americans have taken on more and more debt—mostly through mortgages and other home loans, but through other forms as well. But just because people have high levels of debt does not mean they can't afford to pay the required interest. While record levels of debt suggest that Americans have accumulated excessive amounts, the greater concerns are these: Are Americans able to pay off their debts? Are they resorting to loans requiring higher interest rates? Are they accumulating debt with future benefits for themselves, or is the record debt more an indication of a desperate struggle to get by?

Consumer Credit Is a Convenient Financial Resource for Responsible Borrowers

Virginia Postrel

Virginia Postrel is a contributing editor to The Atlantic. *She hosts a blog at* deepglamour.net.

A couple of weeks after last Christmas [2007], a newspaper reporter telephoned Todd Zywicki, a George Mason University law professor who studies bankruptcy and consumer credit. How, she wanted to know, were American families going to pay the huge credit-card bills they'd run up buying presents? Well, Zywicki responded, how had they paid their Christmas bills the previous year, and the year before that, and the year before that? "It never occurred to her that this was an old story," he says.

Or, as we in the journalism business call it, an evergreen: always in season. Through good times and bad, Americans predictably rack up consumer debt, and that debt predictably generates public and private hand-wringing about how it will ever get paid. When two Federal Reserve economists examined all the *New York Times* articles on consumer credit from 1950 to 1995, they found that 60 percent were negative. The pessimistic tilt was even greater—topping 80 percent—when journalists generated their own stories rather than reporting on statements by politicians, business executives, or academics.

The evergreen story of people in debt becomes even sexier in an economic downturn, when debts inevitably get harder to pay. Witness a recent *Times* feature on "The Debt Trap," described as "a series about the surge in consumer debt and the lenders who made it possible." On the subject of credit, bad news sells.

Virginia Postrel, "The Case for Debt," *The Atlantic*, November 2008, pp. 44, 46–47. Reproduced by permission of the author.

Certainly politicians think so. "Over the past 15 years, average household credit-card debt has tripled. The typical family is now nearly $10,000 in the red," said Barack Obama, decrying a "debt crisis" caused by "credit-card companies ... pushing [consumers] over the edge." At hearings last December, Senator Norm Coleman, the Minnesota Republican, declared, "This easy credit has gotten a lot of people in trouble." He could have said the same thing anytime in the past century and been applauded for it. Today's sluggish economy, home-equity-line-of-credit craze, and subprime-mortgage mess have amplified concerns about the general level of indebtedness. But while it's true that, thanks in large part to declining home prices, American homeowners hold less equity in their homes than they used to, the subprime meltdown is less a problem of consumer credit than of new financial instruments and the difficulty of tracking mortgages that have been sold, then broken up and repackaged into derivative securities. And on closer examination, what looks like "unprecedented" consumer indebtedness turns out to have ample precedent, as do the anxiety and moralizing that accompany it.

Today's sluggish economy, home-equity-line-of-credit craze, and subprime-mortgage mess have amplified concerns about the general level of indebtedness.

Concerns About Excessive Debt Are Nothing New

Studying "Middletown" in the 1920s, Robert S. Lynd and Helen Merrell Lynd deplored the "rise and spread of the dollar-down-and-so-much-per plan," which extended credit for such extravagances as cars, electric washing machines, and "$200 over-stuffed living-room suites ... to persons of whom frequently little is known as to their intention or ability to pay." In 1943, Jesse Rainsford Sprague, a defender of installment buying, nonetheless worried that the "temptations of easy credit" were luring young people to take out bank loans, rather than save, for vacations. Of one stenographer, he noted, "Had the young lady spent less on lip rouge and blood-red fingernail paint, she might have been in a position to pay cash for her holiday."

"As the result of the consumer credit explosion, the total private debt is certainly greater than the combined private debt of man throughout history. Never have so many owed so much," declared Hillel Black in *Buy Now, Pay Later*, published in 1961—more than a decade before using bank credit cards like MasterCard and Visa became common. Employing the big, scary numbers and dizzying examples typical of such critiques, Black elaborated:

> Currently about one hundred million Americans are participating in the buy-now, pay-later binge. Furthermore, they can, if they wish, do anything and everything on credit. Babies are being born on the installment plan, children go through college on time, even funerals are paid for on what the English quaintly call "the never never." Through debt people are buying hairpins, toothpaste, mink coats, girdles, tickets to baseball games, religious medallions, hi-fi equipment, safaris in Africa . . . The result has been a consumer credit explosion that makes the population explosion seem small by comparison.

Technological Advances Have Created New Opportunities

Black was right about the trend but wrong about its significance. The expansion of consumer credit is one of the great economic achievements of the past century. One institutional and technological innovation after another has made borrowing easier and cheaper for rich and poor alike. With each development have come fears—sometimes fueled by the unforeseen problems that inevitably accompany new practices—that *this* is the change that surely will lead to disaster. Yet a half century after Black's warnings, doomsday has not arrived, the "consumer-credit explosion" continues, and most consumers are much better off.

Gone are the up-front fees and intrusive interviews that used to be standard before taking out personal bank loans or establishing store credit. Except for those offering airline miles, most credit cards no longer have annual fees, while intense competition for new customers—think of all that annoying junk mail—has driven down the average interest rate, from 17.4 percent in 1992 to 13.1 percent in 2007. Today's consumer credit is flexible, convenient, impersonal, and (excluding car loans and mortgages) largely unsecured. With a credit card, you can rent a $40,000 automobile, buy goods online from complete strangers, finance a business, make ends meet while you're out of work, purchase a $5,000 wedding gown or a 10-cent photocopy—all without completing any forms or explaining yourself to anyone. And despite recent legal revisions, even bankruptcy is less painful than in the days of buying on time. If you default on your Visa bill, nobody comes to repossess your refrigerator or auction off your shoes. The biggest penalty you'll face is trouble getting future credit.

Easy Credit Fosters Guilt

So why do we worry so much? For starters, the very success of consumer credit makes us uncomfortable. As borrowers, we may feel guilty about running up debt, anxious about making payments, and resentful of the constraints that old obligations (and old credit records) impose on our current choices. We may find it too easy to buy things we may later regret. In theory at least, we might prefer the days when paternalistic—or snobby—salesclerks checked our spending. "Our store manager's duty is to protect the buyer from unwise expenditures," wrote the retailer Julian Goldman in 1930.

If a woman patron selects a gown or a wrap which is beyond her means, the store manager advises against the purchase. He knows, because the customer—conforming to the rule from which there is no deviation—has confidentially explained her circumstances in full detail ... The friendly, intimate, patient, personal interview is the key to our sales operation.

On second thought, why should your economic choices be the store manager's business? Practicality aside, anonymous databases and credit scores are a lot less intrusive.

Almost half the growth in debt between 1989 and 2004 ... came from the highest-income 20 percent of American households.

When credit is cheaper to use and easier to arrange, people do use more of it. Hence those big, scary numbers, which grow along with the economy and the population. Contrary to a common perception, however, the people driving up the totals aren't primarily the financially strapped. They're "high-wealth consumers in their prime earning years," observes Andrew Kish, an economist at the Philadelphia Federal Reserve [Fed]. Almost half the growth in debt between 1989 and 2004 (the most recent year for which data are available) came from the highest-income 20 percent of American households. (By contrast, the bottom 20 percent held about 3 percent of consumer debt—an increase from 1.9 percent—and accounted for a bare 4.5 percent of the growth.) If the rich are getting richer, it makes sense that they're also running up more debt. They can reasonably expect to pay it.

These affluent families also account for half of the outstanding consumer debt. So the $10,000 average that Obama cited isn't in fact owed by the "typical" family with an average income. That figure is calculated by spreading the much larger debts of the rich over the population as a whole. All by herself, Cindy McCain owed at least $200,000 on two American Express cards, according to her husband's [2008 presidential candidate John McCain] campaign disclosure documents. That sounds terrifying until you realize that this wealthy woman pays her monthly AmEx bills in full.

Financial innovations have also made lower-cost credit more available to lower-income people. Even those much-criticized payday loans cost less than pawnshop loans or bounced-check fees. Credit cards are cheaper still.

Government Statistics Skew the Debt Problem

Like those of Mrs. McCain, some of the credit-card balances included in government statistics aren't really debt at all. They're temporary charges for convenience's sake. Nowadays, credit cards are easier to use than cash—no fumbling for change while other shoppers wait impatiently behind you. Plus, companies offer rewards points and frequent-flier miles, and they give you a free float period if you pay your balance in full. So people who don't need to borrow money use their credit cards as a convenience, running up charges over the course of a month and paying everything off when the bill comes due. Whatever they owe on the day that debt statistics are collected goes into the total figures on consumer credit. This "convenience use" grew from about 6 percent of total credit-card debt in 1992 to 11 percent in 2001, calculates Kathleen Johnson, a Fed economist. That growth was two and a half times the growth rate for credit-card borrowing overall.

Of course, rich people and families who pay their bills every month aren't the only Americans with debts, and they certainly aren't the ones whose sad stories make the news. But financial innovations have also made lower-cost credit more available to lower-income people. Even those much-criticized payday loans cost less than pawnshop loans or bounced-check fees. Credit cards are cheaper still.

Credit Cards Are Both Convenient and Confusing

And credit-card companies have changed their lending policies in ways that make credit more accessible—but also more complicated. Credit-card prices used to be "high and simple," notes another study by the Philadelphia Fed. Everybody paid the same rate, regardless of credit risk. If you carried a balance but reliably paid your bills, you were subsidizing borrowers who weren't so dependable. But because the interest rate wasn't high enough to cover the riskiest potential customers, generally those with lower incomes or frequent unemployment, they were cut out of the credit-card market altogether.

Now, instead of charging everyone the same, companies adjust the interest rates according to customers' credit scores. They also charge special fees for late payments, purchases that exceed a credit limit, foreign-currency transactions, phone payments, and so forth. This structure makes it profitable to extend credit to high-risk borrowers, including those with low incomes. It's more inclusive, and arguably fairer, since it eliminates cross-subsidies. But it's also hard to explain. Hence Obama's complaints that credit-card contracts "have gone from being one page long a few decades ago to more than 30 pages long today."

Of course, in the good old days of one-page contracts, politicians still decried easy credit and demanded more consumer information. Ever wonder why your credit-card agreement's easy-to-read "Schumer Box" specifies a minimum finance charge of, say, 50 cents? You've probably never thought twice about that charge, but back in the late 1980s, then-Congressman Charles Schumer and his colleagues thought that telling consumers the minimum charge was very important.

And back in those good old days, of course, some people still couldn't make their credit-card payments. Others worried that they'd never get out of debt. Still others felt guilty about buying luxuries even when they could afford them. Forms of credit may change, but credit anxiety, alas, does not.

The Majority of Borrowers Live Within Their Financial Means

John Zogby

John Zogby is president and CEO of Zogby International, a polling firm that has been tracking public opinion around the world since 1984. He also is the author of The Way We'll Be: The Zogby Report on the Transformation of the American Dream.

It's no secret that Americans have become addicted to credit in order to maintain an artificially high standard of living. According to a recent CardTrak.com survey of 55,000 consumers, 13% of Americans have credit card balances of more than $25,000.

Have we lost our way when it comes to credit? Now celebrating my 25th year as a pollster, I've learned to read statistics with a bit of dyslexia, taking a look at them backward and upside down. So I discovered that almost half of that 13% were people who could well afford to carry that much credit card debt—which meant to me that approximately nine in 10 Americans were living within their means with regard to credit card debt. The real truth here is that most Americans are living their lives modestly, but this does not make a dramatic headline.

Most Americans Are Not Overextended

But Americans have bought into the misconception that most of us are overextended. Taking into account a household's overall financial picture, a Zogby Interactive survey conducted in March 2008 found that 79% of Americans believe they themselves live within their means financially, given their current personal financial situation.

This same survey found that 87% believe that most other Americans are living beyond their financial means. Our more recent polling shows Americans have been trimming their budgets in response to today's financial reality—on entertainment, major purchases, even groceries. The Great Recession has not created a new mindset, because it was already here.

It's not so much that we're a nation of debtors—though there are a lot of us with too much debt—but that we're not a nation of savers. On the surface, it would appear that Americans have an insatiable appetite for things they cannot afford. *The Economist* reported in 2008 that household and consumer debt was up from 100% of gross domestic product in 1980 to 173% by 2007.

But consider the reality that much new debt has been caused by students who graduate from college with unmanageable credit card payments, and that a substantial burden is being carried by these college graduates well into their thirties. Much of this growing debt is in start-up costs for young people and added penalties and interest rates.

Consumers Are Changing Their Attitudes About Credit

There are many of us working for less, and many who have come to the realization that they cannot achieve the American Dream on a buy-now pay-later basis. The Great Recession is not creating a new trend but rather accelerating one I have noted over the last decade: a move away from easy credit, away from buying what we can't afford, away from seeking out fantasy.

We can see new evidence of this movement as the nation's personal savings rate hit a 14-year high of 5% in January [2009], and as consumer spending continues to lag.

Our May 2008 polling found only 17% of Americans planned to spend any portion of their federal tax rebate check on a spending "splurge." Instead, Americans were much more focused on using most of their rebate to pay down credit card bills and other loans (30%), pay for everyday expenses such as gas, food and utilities (24%), or for savings (21%).

My polling has found that more people believe the American Dream is about spiritual fulfillment (39%) than about material success (35%). Evidence of this movement was found throughout our consumer survey in April 2005, including that twice as many Americans rated "a simple evening at home with loved ones" more highly on a "pleasure scale" as they did "an elegant evening in a pricey restaurant."

It takes more than a recession to change the soul of a nation, and our polling shows Americans are becoming increasingly conscious about their spending. A Zogby Interactive survey in February 2009 showed 70% have cut back on entertainment, recreation, and eating out at restaurants—including those with the greatest household income. These include the 9 million to 10 million Americans who are doing well financially but have concluded that they not only have enough, but they actually have too much.

This country is moving away from overspending and overuse of credit.

A Movement Toward Moderation

This is all part of a growing movement toward simplification. A General Social Survey analysis of Americans' satisfaction with their financial situation has remained remarkably high and consistent for the past 35 years—in 2006, 76% were "pretty well satisfied" or "more or less satisfied," compared with 73% in 1996, 74% in 1986, and 77% in 1979. This is despite an increase in income inequality and knowing that 27%

of us are working for less—yet people seem to be adjusting to their changing financial circumstances.

This country is moving away from overspending and overuse of credit. Surveys since the recession began show Americans modifying their expectations even more. An annual survey held during the holiday shopping season showed 71% planned to spend less due to the weakening economy. Once the economy turns—and it will—look for less binging and less demand for 0% APRs [annual percentage rates of interest] today that turn into 32% APRs tomorrow.

CHAPTER 2

Are Credit Cards Good for Consumers?

Overview: The History and Function of the Credit Card

Federal Deposit Insurance Corporation

The Federal Deposit Insurance Corporation (FDIC) is an independent agency created by the U.S. Congress to maintain stability and public confidence in the nation's financial system.

In its non-physical form, a credit card represents a payment mechanism which facilitates both consumer and commercial business transactions, including purchases and cash advances. A credit card generally operates as a substitute for cash or a check and most often provides an unsecured revolving line of credit. The borrower is required to pay at least part of the card's outstanding balance each billing cycle, depending on the terms as set forth in the cardholder agreement. As the debt reduces, the available credit increases for accounts in good standing. These complex financial arrangements have ever-shifting terms and prices. A charge card differs from a credit card in that the charge card must be paid in full each month.

In physical form, a credit card traditionally is a thin, rectangular plastic card. The front of the card contains a series of numbers that are representative of various items such as the applicable network, bank, and account. These numbers are generally referred to in aggregate as the account number or card number. A magnetic stripe, often called a magstripe, runs across the back of the card and contains some of the account's information electronically. The back of the card also contains a cardholder signature box. There are many other physical attributes to a credit card; however, as technologies progress, their physical form is morphing. For example, multi-

Federal Deposit Insurance Corporation (FDIC), "Chapter 2: Credit Cards—General Overview," *Credit Card Activities Manual*. Washington, D.C.: Federal Deposit Insurance Corporation, 2007.

application cards (sometimes referred to as smart cards) involve aspects of cryptography (secret codes) and, in place of the magstripe, have a microprocessor, or chip, built into the card. The enhanced memory and processing capacity greatly exceeds that of the traditional magstripe card, and the multi-application cards can enable consumers to access several financial accounts and other services or data (like merchant loyalty programs) with a single card. Emerging formats also include contactless and biometric payment options. With the contactless payment format, cards are tapped on readers (instead of swiped) at the point-of-sale. This format is also known as proximity, "tap 'n go," or blink technology. The biometric format relies on a cardholder's physical or biological features by using identification techniques like fingerprint verification, iris scans, or voice scans. Electronic payment innovations may well be only in their infancy.

The Credit Card Industry Is Marked by Intense Competition

The credit card lending business experiences rapid change, but not just in the technology environment. New competitors continue to emerge from not only the banking industry, but from phone companies, retailers and others. At the same time, consolidation among credit card issuers has also increased. For example, during a four-month period in 2005, the three largest monoline credit card banks, (MBNA, Capital One Financial Corporation, and Providian) all announced some type of acquisition transactions.

The credit card industry's focus has shifted from prestige to merchant acceptance to pricing and perks. Intense competition, market saturation, and changing consumer postures have forced issuers to be innovative with the credit card products offered and to develop sophisticated customer selection and management methods. Processes have evolved to risk ranking applicants and pricing each account accordingly. Risk-based pricing has allowed banks to issue cards to less-qualified applicants in exchange for a higher interest rate or other fees and to essentially offer customized card products. Rewards programs are extremely popular, and credit cards can now be used to purchase items in well over 100 currencies.

Visa and MasterCard (together referred to as Associations) quickly come to mind when the term "credit card" is used. Traditionally banks purchased memberships in the Associations, and, in return, receive the right to offer credit card products or other services under the applicable Association's logo. In addition to operating worldwide sophisticated payment networks, the Associations provide services including, but not limited to, advertising, statistical analysis, industry studies, and advisory services. They require their member banks to be insured and to operate within certain policies. The Associations do not issue cards or financial services directly to consumers or merchants. Rather, they focus on advancing payment products and technologies for their member banks, and the member banks manage the relationships with consumers and merchants. The Associations offer various membership grades, which can be subject to certain requirements, such as capital levels or acceptable growth projections.

The credit card industry's focus has shifted from prestige to merchant acceptance to pricing and perks.

While the Associations remain the prominent brands in the bank credit card industry, other brands, such as American Express and Discover, are challenging their share. Unlike the Associations, American Express and Discover traditionally both issued their own cards. While they have long been in the credit card business, they only recently expanded their access within the bank credit card business as a result of court rulings in 2004. Those rulings said that the Associations' policies barring member banks from contracting with American Express and Discover violated antitrust rules. The rulings have not only resulted in some Visa and MasterCard banks now also offering American Express and/or Discover cards, but are also leading to dual-branding. For simplicity, MasterCard, Visa, American Express, and Discover are collectively referred to as Networks in this [essay]. The term Networks is used because these companies interconnect a large and widely distributed group of people and entities to communicate with one another and work together as a system to facilitate card transactions. The system allows for the routing of a transaction's information between the participants in a matter of fractions of a second.

The legal and regulatory environment for the bank credit card industry continues to shape the industry as well. For instance, in the 1970's, the U.S. Supreme Court ruled that the lender's location, not the consumer's state of residence, determined the applicable state usury ceiling. As a result, large card issuers have sought out states with lender-friendly usury ceilings in which to establish national operations. For example, several bank credit card operations are located in South Dakota and Delaware. The 1970's also saw Congress enact a number of consumer credit protection laws. More recent banking regulatory developments include the issuance of subprime lending guidance in 1999 and 2001 and account management and loss allowance guidance in 2003.

Card Types and Attributes

A multitude of credit card products are available to consumers, and the number of products is growing. Terms and conditions of each credit card product offered, such as the Annual Percentage Rate (APR), the monthly minimum payment formula, and certain fees, are detailed in a cardholder agreement, which is required by regulation. The following sections provide an overview of some common credit card product categories.

General purpose, or universal, credit cards can be used at a variety of stores and businesses. They take on many forms, including standard, premium, affinity, co-branded, corporate, home equity, and cash secured programs, each of which is briefly described next.

Over-reliance on the premium sector creates the potential of greater losses in the event high outstanding balances exist during an economic downturn.

Standard Credit Card Programs: Standard credit card programs are a traditional form of credit card issuance. These programs are usually marketed to consumers who meet or exceed the institution's minimum credit criteria but that may lack sufficient credit history or may fail to meet some of the institution's other credit criteria. Due to the higher credit risk and loss rates, these programs generally carry higher interest rates, higher fees, and lower credit limits than premium credit card programs. In addition to cash secured credit cards (discussed later), unsecured standard credit card programs are frequently used for providing credit to subprime borrowers [people with low credit scores or limited credit history].

Premium Credit Card Programs: Premium credit card programs tend to be marketed to consumers that have higher income and/or higher credit scores than those consumers offered standard credit cards. Premium programs have traditionally consisted of gold and platinum credit cards. However, some issuers have moved toward using these premium-sounding titles with more standard-type products to combat strong competition and entice consumers to opt for their cards. Premium credit card programs usually carry lower interest rates, waived annual fees, and higher credit limits. The risk with this type of program is a large volume of high-balance accounts. Over-reliance on the premium sector creates the potential of greater losses in the event high outstanding balances exist during an economic downturn.

Affinity Credit Card Programs: Affinity relationships are partnerships formed between financial institutions and unaffiliated groups (affinity partners), generally nonprofit organizations such as, but not limited to, alumni associations, professional organizations, and fan clubs. A contractual agreement governs the relationship with the affinity partner, and the affinity cards issued usually carry the affinity partner's logo. Compensation varies, but the affinity partner endorsing the card usually receives financial compensation based on the projected level of acceptance and use by its members. Compensation often comes in the form of the sharing of annual fees, renewal fees, interchange income, and interest income. Issuers seek affinity endorsements to increase response, usage, and retention rates.

Co-branded Credit Card Programs: Co-branded relationships are partnerships formed between financial institutions and unaffiliated organizations, generally for-profit organizations such as airlines, automobile manufacturers, and retailers. Similar to the affinity program, a contractual agreement governs the co-branded relationship, and the co-branded card usually carries the co-branded partner's logo. Compensation to the co-branding partner often takes the form of sharing interchange fees and/or rebates to its customers. Rebates to customers are normally based on a percentage of purchases or transactions, and the percentage often varies depending on whether purchases were made with the co-branding party or another entity. The institution benefits from a co-branding arrangement because it generally increases credit card receivables, and accordingly interest and interchange income, due to the consumers' willingness to use the credit card more frequently to reap the financial rewards. However, institutions typically face the risk that higher cardholder monthly payment rates could erode profits. Nevertheless, for some programs, the considerable volume of interchange income generated by high cardholder transaction volumes might substantially offset the interest income opportunity that is lost with higher payment rates.

Corporate Credit Card Programs: Corporate card programs come in more than one form to serve different business needs. In general, they are contractual agreements between a sponsoring entity and a financial institution, in which the financial institution issues corporate cards to select employees of the sponsoring company. The sponsoring entities may take on several forms including small businesses; middle market businesses; local, state, or Federal governments; and large corporations. With this type of program, examiners should determine if the institution is allowed to make commercial loans. While most banks are permitted to make commercial loans, others are prohibited by state law or charter restrictions.

Travel and entertainment (T&E) cards are used for business functions such as travel, lodging, and entertainment. The contract identifies the repayment terms and whether the sponsoring company guarantees the loans. These terms often dictate how the bank sets the credit limits.

Co-branded relationships are partnerships formed between financial institutions and unaffiliated organizations, generally for-profit organizations such as airlines, automobile manufacturers, and retailers.

Procurement cards are used for a business's purchases of materials, office supplies, and miscellaneous items. Businesses are attracted to this product because it simplifies accounting, especially for small-ticket items. Purchase orders are not needed, and only one payables check is necessary. In addition, institutions can provide value-added features such as detailed account statements and summary statistical information on purchasing patterns. The ability to provide value-added features is a critical competitive factor between institutions. Depending on the needs of the corporation these accounts may have credit limits in the millions of dollars.

Corporate card accounts generally pay monthly; thus, issuing banks normally forego finance charges, which could make past due accounts very costly to the bank. The primary source of income on these accounts consists of service fees, annual fees, and interchange income.

Home Equity Credit Card Programs: Home equity credit cards are secured by housing assets. These credit cards provide consumers with the benefits of a traditional home equity line of credit (attractive interest rates and potential tax deductibility) while allowing them quick, easy access to the line's funds via the credit card. Home equity credit card lending involves a significant amount of documentation due to the mortgages, insurances, and other aspects involved. Points unique to these programs compared to unsecured programs include loan-to-value (LTV) and foreclosure considerations.

Cash Secured Credit Card Programs: Cash secured credit cards are generally marketed to two consumers groups: those with poor credit scores or prior credit problems and those with a limited or non-existent credit history. These programs can allow consumers an opportunity to establish or re-establish their credit. The accounts are collateralized by savings accounts or certificates of deposits. Cash secured credit card lending can be profitable and attractive to institutions because the receivables are self funding, finance charges and fees are high, the collateral is liquid, and new markets are opened.

Other Types of Credit Cards

Proprietary cards, also called private label cards, are issued under a contractual agreement between financial institutions and third parties, usually large retailers, for the purpose of consumers transacting business with that entity. Some are also issued by the retailers and do not involve a financial institution. Private label cards often exhibit different traits than general purpose cards in that private label cards normally have lower credit limits, higher interest rates, higher credit risk profiles, and limited use (for example, limited to a particular merchant). There is risk of the retail partner failing. While significant direct exposure to the company may not be evident, high losses may still result if cardholders do not feel compelled to repay outstanding balances. Some customers may not honor obligations due to lost warranties or rights to return merchandise. Others might not repay the debt simply because the merchant is no longer in business. In either case, the bankruptcy of a retail partner usually creates a significant collection problem. In addition, credit risk is closely correlated with the traits of the cardholder population which are usually small, niche markets tending to have volatile performance patterns. The credit quality of these populations also tends to be lower because there is generally an incentive to establish liberal underwriting standards and enroll as many applicants as possible to generate business for the retail partner.

Cash access credit cards are marketed to consumers who tend to prefer cash advances over purchases. These cards are not used for traditional point-of-sale transactions. Cash-users are typically considered a higher-risk population. In some cases these borrowers may be using cash advances to pay debts, including balances on this or other credit cards (this can also be true for some borrowers who use cash advance features of their general purpose cards).

Not all cards issued by banks are credit cards. For example, banks also issue debit cards and prepaid or stored value cards. Examples of stored-value cards include payroll cards, electronic benefits transfer (EBT) cards, travel fund cards, and store gift cards.

Most Consumers Owe Little or Nothing to Credit Card Companies

Liz Pulliam Weston

Liz Pulliam Weston is a personal finance columnist for MSN Money *and author of the question-and-answer column* Money Talk, *which appears in newspapers throughout the country. She is the author of* Easy Money: How to Simplify Your Finances and Get What You Want Out of Life, Deal with Your Debt, *and* Your Credit Score: How to Fix, Protect and Improve the 3-Digit Number That Shapes Your Financial Future.

You've probably heard that the average American carries more than $8,000 in credit card debt.

It's a figure frequently cited by politicians, journalists, and pundits as a sure sign of impending economic collapse. They argue that consumers, already struggling under this massive burden of debt, soon will have to stop spending like drunken sailors. The economic recovery, therefore, is doomed!

The surprising thing about this statistic isn't that it's so widely known. Rather, it's that the statistic paints a picture that's just plain wrong.

- In reality, most Americans owe nothing to credit card companies.

- Most households that carry balances owe $2,000 or less.

- Only about 1 in 20 American households owes $8,000 or more on credit cards.

These figures are from the Federal Reserve's [Fed's] 2001 Survey of Consumer Finances, one of the most comprehensive

Liz Pulliam Weston, "The Truth About Credit Card Debt," *MSN Money* (money.msn.com), April 23, 2006. Reproduced by permission of the author.

assessments of what Americans own and owe. (The survey is updated every three years; a summary of 2004's results will be published in early 2006.)

Using Averages Is Misleading

Most of the people citing the $8,000 figure credit it to Card Web.com, a service that tracks credit card trends.

CardWeb, however, doesn't contend that the average American owes more than $8,000 on cards. Their statistics show that the average *debt* per American household with at least one credit card was $8,940 in 2002, the last year for which figures are available.

If you know anything about statistics, however, you know that averages don't really tell the tale.

To get that number, CardWeb simply divided the total outstanding credit card debt at the end of 2002—$750.9 billion—by the 84 million American households that it says have at least one credit card. (CardWeb uses a slightly different definition of household than the Fed does. And the company contends that 80% of households, rather than the Feds 76.2%, have at least one credit card.)

Now, by CardWeb's measure and definition, the average debt in households with at least one credit card *is* growing.

If you know anything about statistics, however, you know that averages don't really tell the tale.

Consider what would happen if you and 17 of your friends and family were in a room with Bill Gates and Warren Buffett. The *average* net worth of a person in that room would be north of $4 billion. The fact that everybody else's *personal* net worth was just $100,000, or $1 million, or even $10 million, wouldn't affect the average that much because the big boys are sooooo much wealthier than you.

Most Borrowers Pay Off Their Monthly Balances

In much the same way, a relatively small population with huge credit card balances can skew the average to make it look like the typical American is carrying a much bigger debt load than he or she actually is. Consider:

- 23.8% of American households have no credit cards at all—no bank cards, no retail cards, nothing.

- Another 31.2% of the households the Fed surveyed paid off their most recent credit card bills in full.

- So together, the households that owed nothing on credit cards equaled 55% of the total.

Here's some better news: Paying off balances actually became more common between 1998 and 2001. The proportion of households that had bank cards (Visa, MasterCard, etc.) who reported that they regularly paid off their balances in full rose 1.5 percentage points to 55.3%.

Only a Small Percentage of Borrowers Carry Excessive Debt

Of the households that did carry a balance, the median amount owed was $1,900. That means half of the households with a balance owed more, and half owed less. (Medians are less subject to the skewing phenomenon that plagues averages; that's why economists tend to favor them.)

Bill Whitt at the VIP Forum, a Washington D.C. research firm, helped me dig even deeper. By analyzing the credit card debts of all the households the Fed surveyed, Whitt discovered:

- Only 29% of households owe $1,000 or more on their cards.

- 21% owe $2,000 or more.

- 6% owe $8,000 or more.

- 4% owe $10,500 or more.

- 1% owe $21,400 or more.

The Fed statistics pretty much gibe with what Fair Isaac [Corp., FICO], the creator of the FICO credit score, discovered when it reviewed millions of credit reports.

There are a few differences between the universe the Fed examined and the one looked at by Fair Isaac. For one thing, credit reports are individual—theres no such thing as a household or even a joint credit report. Also, you have to have and use credit to have a credit report. Finally, credit reports don't typically distinguish between balances you pay off and those you carry each month.

But again, Fair Isaac's statistics show a world in which most people are light to moderate users of credit:

- About 48% of credit card holders owed less than $1,000

- About 10% of card holders had total card balances in excess of $10,000.

- More than half of all people with credit cards use less than 30% of their total credit card limit.

- Just over 1 in 8 people use 80% or more of their credit card limit.

Many Low-Income Americans Do Struggle with Debt

Does this mean all the hand-wringing over consumer debt is so much noise? Hardly. Although most Americans seem to be avoiding the credit card trap, there are still plenty of people on the financial edge:

- More than a third—36%—of those who owe more than $10,000 on their cards have household incomes under $50,000, according to the VIP Forum analysis.

- 13% who owe that much have household incomes under $30,000.

- The percentage of disposable income used to pay debts is still near record highs.

- The median value of total outstanding debt owed by households rose 9.6% between 1998 and 2001.

- Bankruptcies set another record in 2003, with 1.6 million personal filings, the American Bankruptcy Institute reports.

All of that is more than enough evidence to suggest that a large number of people are overdosing on debt. The *average* American, though, seems to be doing just fine.

Credit Cards Allow for Convenient, Secure Financial Transactions

Richard Gilliland

Richard Gilliland writes articles and reviews about the credit card industry for Buzzle.com.

Credit cards may be the easiest way to get a standby line of revolving credit, always available when you need it, but it can also be the fastest way to get mired in credit card debt. People may complain about credit card debt but everyone agrees that despite the risks, there are too many drawbacks to not having a credit card.

Credit cards as we know them today are relatively new and are continuously evolving. The major laws protecting consumers' rights involving credit were passed in the mid-seventies. It may be timely that Congress is currently considering added measures to enhance consumer protection. Yet, for a long time, people were using credit cards as a convenience product rather than as loans. Many people paid their entire balance each month. Credit cards were not as essential then as they are now.

Credit Cards Have Changed from a Convenience to a Necessity

Banks do not make money if people did not carry balances since a grace period for purchases, where no interest is charged for one month, is usually standard. As far as banks are concerned, the best credit card customer is one who carries a balance each month after remitting the minimum payment on time. Credit card issuers got really creative and have managed

Richard Gilliland, "Drawbacks of Not Having a Credit Card," Buzzle.com, July 14, 2007. Reproduced by permission.

to make credit cards a necessary part of daily living. They worked to have credit cards accepted in more and more establishments, and to have credit card holders understand the many benefits and conveniences that they stood to gain from using their credit cards.

In our times, credit cards [are] no longer a luxury. If you travel, you need your credit card to book flight reservations and reserve hotel rooms. You also need credit cards to rent cars, to purchase gas, and buy products by telephone or online. Being without credit cards today would make your life as difficult as traveling by horse and buggy. Without our even being aware of it, credit cards have become a business standard.

As far as banks are concerned, the best credit card customer is one who carries a balance each month after remitting the minimum payment on time.

A credit card is one of the quickest ways to build a credit history. When you apply for a credit card and you still have no history, there are credit card issuers that you can approach. These issuers specialize in providing credit card products to customers who, because they are still attempting to establish or expand their credit history, are generally evaluated as higher credit risks. Many college students, for example, fall into this category, along with those who have limited employment income, or otherwise have poor credit history.

Today, having credit is a necessity. An inexpensive, reliable new car costs thousands of dollars, and although most people may want to pay in cash, the reality is they will need a loan. The rates and terms of that loan will be determined by your credit history, which is easily obtainable from the credit bureaus throughout the country. If you have used credit wisely in the past and repaid previous loans on time, you will be in a favorable position. If not, the result will be a more costly loan with higher interest rates.

Credit Cards Are Now a Part of Everyday Life

The use of the credit card as a source of loans is illustrated by the fact that overall credit card debt now runs several hundred billions of dollars. Credit card debt has risen quickly to unimaginable proportions, and still banks continue to compete heavily for your business. Every year, billions of credit card flyers with invitations to transfer to another card issuer are sent out. The average American credit card holder is now in possession of almost a dozen credit cards, with average debt of $13,000. The credit card has indeed become a cornerstone of everyday living. Other than its necessity in making flight and hotel reservations, credit cards help the credit card holder with:

- "Cashless" transactions that avoid the risk of carrying around too much cash

- An interest-free loan from the time of purchase until the payment is due

- Cash advances from an ATM, in emergency cases

- The ability to shop by telephone or online

- The ability to purchase items when cash is not sufficient

- The ability to withhold payment when dissatisfied with a purchase or to dispute erroneous billings

- An instant source of credit that is available without filling out forms or undergoing further credit checks.

Cash, when it gets lost, is irretrievable; unlike cash, if you lose your credit card you can get a replacement no matter where you are. You also get protection against fraud or unauthorized use, which means you have minimal or even zero liability. Credit cards can be a resource in case of emergencies, such as a large car repair bill or an unforeseen expense.

Credit card companies normally provide the card holders with copies of their monthly statements. These statements list down in detail all charges that have been made against your credit card account. The monthly statements can thus serve as a complete financial record which, to the prudent credit card user, can become a guide for budgeting and controlling expenses. If the card user is a student, the monthly statements can become a tool for learning financial responsibility. Indeed, for personal finances and small businesses, credit cards have become a necessary financial tool.

There is also the prospect of being able to save money on future transactions because the usual credit card offers a number of rewards privileges that include frequent flyer miles, cash rebates, discounts or free telephone calls, points that go toward reduction of the cost of airplane tickets and hotel stays, points that can be redeemed as consumer products or gift certificates. All of the major credit cards—Visa, Master-Card, American Express—offer a multitude of card products with endless permutations on rewards, benefits, and privileges that you can enjoy to maximize the value you get from your credit cards.

Unlike cash, if you lose your credit card you can get a replacement no matter where you are.

Credit Card Holders Have Responsibilities

Ownership of a credit card entails certain responsibilities on your part. If these responsibilities are not exercised dutifully, you could unwittingly put yourself in a difficult situation where you lose your credit card privileges and suffer the drawbacks of not having credit cards. Your primary responsibilities as a credit card holder include the obligation to pay your bills on time, to stay within your pre-set spending limit, and to maintain the worthiness of your credit.

The convenience of having credit cards may tempt you to live beyond your means. You need to remember that excessive credit card debt and late payments will impair your credit rating and make it more difficult and costly to obtain credit in the future. Remember it is very easy to lower your credit ratings, but painfully slow to raise it.

It is now more important than ever to be effective at managing credit card debt. This is particularly true for people living from paycheck-to-paycheck and who must dip into their credit sources to make ends meet. If you are able to plan your credit spending and payments to your account, you will be rewarded with higher lines of credit and better rates. Otherwise, if you're not efficient and disciplined with your credit card, you'll have very few options available.

Credit Card Technology Spurs Domestic and International Economic Growth

Scott Schmith

Scott Schmith is an international trade specialist in the U.S. Department of Commerce's International Trade Administration.

Growth in the electronic payments sector has surpassed general economic growth and growth in other financial sectors. Electronic payments include credit, debit, and other electronic instruments used to transfer payments from consumers to merchants. This [essay] will use the terms *"electronic payments"* and *"credit cards"* interchangeably but will refer explicitly to credit cards when discussing empirical studies limited to credit card payments.

The growth in the electronic payments sector is accompanied by numerous economic and transactional benefits. As demonstrated by Muhammad Yunus and the Grameen Bank, winners of the 2006 Nobel Peace Prize, gains from financial innovations can be extensive, widespread, and developmentally favorable. Electronic payments improve economic inefficiencies, make payments more secure and convenient, and, as a corollary to the lessons learned from microfinance, provide the impetus for further economic and social development.

For developing countries, those gains could be significant, but they would depend on the concurrent development of the appropriate network and payments infrastructure, government regulation, consumer education, and competition within the sector. As governments in developed economies have learned, adequate regulatory oversight in the electronic payments sector is essential to maintaining financial stability, consumer

Scott Schmith, "Credit Card Market: Economic Benefits and Industry Trends," U.S. Department of Commerce, International Trade Administration, Washington, D.C.: 2008.

confidence, and data privacy and security of the sector. Although electronic payments growth could represent an opportunity for developing countries to rebalance their economies by encouraging domestic consumption—and an opportunity for the United States to lower its trade deficit—governments, industry, and consumer groups will need to educate consumers to use electronic payments responsibly and securely.

This [essay] will first discuss how electronic payments promote economic efficiency and growth. Second, it will describe additional benefits for consumers and merchants. Third, it will show how the financial sector and electronic payments enhance economic growth and innovation. Fourth, it will discuss how electronic payments affect exports. Fifth, it will discuss credit card market penetration in selected countries. Next, it will discuss a forecast for the electronic payments market. Finally, it will discuss the infrastructure required for building a successful payment network.

Electronic Payments Promote Economic Efficiency and Growth

Electronic payments expand the consumer market, increase banking access to the unbanked, improve macroeconomic efficiency, and encourage entrepreneurial activity. The ultimate benefit of adapting an electronic payments system will depend on how competition and the evolution of the informal sector affect how widely electronic payments are adopted.

Electronic Payments Expand the Consumer Market. The development of an electronic payments system enlarges the consumer market and boosts the purchase of U.S. exports, particularly in the e-commerce and travel and tourism sectors. According to an analysis of a cross-section of 50 countries by Global Insight, increasing the existing share of electronic payments in a country by a margin of just 10 percent will generate an increase of 0.5 percent in consumer spending. For example, according to the Economist Intelligence Unit, consumer expenditure in China was $865 billion in 2005. Increasing credit cards' share of the transaction market from 20 percent to 22 percent would result in an incremental $4.33 billion in consumer expenditure.

Electronic Payments Increase Access to the Banking System. Electronic payments act as gateways into the banking system for unbanked segments, which make up as much as 70 percent of the world's population. In a simulation of the U.S. economy, a 10 percent shift of currency into deposits or other reserves that can be used for loans increased GDP [gross domestic product] by more than 1 percent annually. Many Latin American countries, such as Brazil and Mexico, with large unbanked or underbanked populations would benefit significantly from movements into the formal financial sector.

Electronic Payments Create Macroeconomic Efficiency. Electronic payment networks have the potential to provide cost savings of at least 1 percent of GDP annually over paper-based systems through increased velocity, reduced friction, and lower costs. For China, with a nominal—that is, unadjusted for purchasing power parity (PPP)—GDP of $2.278 trillion in 2005, that amount translates into a potential savings of roughly $23 billion.

Electronic payments expand the consumer market, increase banking access to the unbanked, improve macroeconomic efficiency, and encourage entrepreneurial activity.

Electronic Payments Are a Source of Capital for Start-ups. Credit cards are one of the most reliable sources of start-up funds for new entrepreneurs. Unlike bank loan officers, private angel investors, or government lending programs, credit cards offer a simple and rapid access to capital that has helped a significant number of U.S. entrepreneurs establish new businesses. In addition, factoring future credit card receipts for short-term capital needs is a valuable option for many small businesses. The small and medium-sized enterprise sector in emerging countries, which typically has difficulty accessing financing, could benefit from that alternative financing source.

Electronic Payments Benefit Consumers and Merchants

In addition to the numerous economic benefits that result from expanding the electronic payments markets, electronic payments systems also provide consumer and seller protection and convenience.

For consumers, electronic payments provide an established system of dispute resolution, increase the security of their payments, and reduce their liability for stolen or misused cards. Electronic payments also provide immediate access to funds on deposit through debit cards and offer the convenience of global acceptance, a wide range of payment options, and enhanced financial management tools.

For sellers, electronic payments improve the speed and security of the transaction processing chain, from verification and authorization to clearing and settlement. Such payments also provide better management of cash flow, inventory, and financial planning through rapid bank payments. Electronic payments may also reduce costs and risks by eliminating the need to run an in-house credit facility.

Financial Sector Development Enhances Economic Growth and Innovation

Financial development increases economic growth by directing capital to an economy's most productive areas. The greater a country's financial development, the larger the economic growth over the subsequent decades. A doubling of the size of private credit in a developing country is associated with a 2 percent annual increase in economic growth. Finally, more new firms are created in countries with developed financial systems, and capital-dependent industries and firms grow faster.

The development of the financial system includes the banking, securities, and electronic payments sectors. Electronic payments, for example, contribute toward the development of a more efficient and sound financial system. Numerous studies show that the growth of electronic payments has measurable economic benefits for countries primarily because electronic payments are much more cost-effective on a large scale than cash payments. E-commerce and travel and tourism, for example, are two sectors that depend significantly on the ability of consumers to use electronic payments at the point of purchase.

Electronic Payments and Exports

In addition to its role in developing a country's domestic economy, the electronic payments sector is also linked to an expansion of exports. As discussed earlier, more accessible and convenient payment options facilitate larger consumer purchases. An analysis of credit card penetration data shows a moderate correlation between credit cards per capita and exports per capita, which is higher than the correlation between GDP per capita and exports per capita. Also, a moderate correlation exists between changes in credit card penetration and exports. Although it is likely that both credit card penetration and exports between 1998 and 2005 were affected by economic growth in GDP, that analysis suggests that the development of electronic payments markets has important implications for further economic and trade opportunities for U.S. businesses.

Credit Card Market Penetration in Selected Countries Is Growing

[There are] . . . six important trends or characteristics [of credit card market penetration]:

1. More developed countries generally have higher card penetration, although there are several examples of less developed countries that have higher usage than more developed countries.

2. Credit card penetration varies widely among countries. The United States, for example, had a penetration of 2.53 cards per capita in 2005 versus only 0.02 cards per capita in India.

3. There has been impressive growth in credit card penetration across income levels and in economic growth. The average growth rate in credit card penetration has greatly exceeded country and global growth for all but a few countries.

4. There is more variation in credit card penetration in Asia than in Latin America or the transitional economies in Eastern Europe (such as the Czech Republic, Hungary, Poland, and Russia).

5. Credit card penetration in the transitional countries has grown faster than in other countries, primarily because of the recent opening of the financial markets in countries that were already enjoying moderate levels of economic development.

The average growth rate in credit card penetration has greatly exceeded country and global growth for all but a few countries.

---

6. The number of credit card companies competing in a country varies significantly, from eight in Russia to one in China. There appears to be a rough correlation between the number of companies and credit card penetration.

Growth Is Forecast for the Global Electronic Payments Market

Global Insight, an economic consultancy, expects a 13.1 percent growth in electronic retail transactions from 2004 to 2009 across 79 countries, supported by global economic growth and the transition from cash and paper transactions to electronic payments. . . . Global Insight predicts that the transitional economies of Eastern Europe are likely to have the highest growth rates, behind India, China, and South Korea. . . . Among emerging regions, Latin America will experience more moderate growth in electronic transactions because its overall economic growth rate is slower and it already has higher credit card penetration rates than other regions, particularly Eastern Europe. Electronic payments usage will depend on economic growth, infrastructure, consumer education, transparency, and regulation.

Successful Electronic Payment Systems Need Strong Infrastructure and Efficient Regulation

The infrastructure needed to support a vibrant electronic payments sector has four components: a telecommunication system, an acceptance network, credit bureaus, and consumer education. In addition, electronic payments require sound and efficient regulation, from both the relevant government bodies and the private payments network.

Telecommunication System. A telecommunication system that can support real-time authorization is essential. Until recently, a sufficient telecommunication system required fixed telephone landlines, but recent innovations in wireless technology permit the development of electronic payments systems in places where they were previously unsustainable.

Acceptance Network. Consumers react most positively to electronic payments when the acceptance infrastructure is widespread and robust. Depending on the target segment, point-of-sale terminals, automatic teller machines, bank branches, and Internet, mail order, or telephone merchants need to be available to accept consumers' cards.

Credit Bureaus. Credit bureaus are necessary to provide accurate and timely credit information to issuing banks. Credit bureaus that cover a wide consumer base, that include positive and negative credit information, that require information sharing, and whose credit information extends for at least two years are integral components of sustainable electronic payments markets. Auxiliary information, such as utility and rent payment timeliness, has recently been used for sectors or markets outside of the traditional credit markets.

Consumer Education. Financial literacy initiatives help to promote safe and responsible banking habits as new payment instruments are introduced. Merchants will need to understand the electronic devices they are using, and institutional buyers will need to develop appropriate procedures and safeguards.

Regulation. A payment system needs common effective operating regulations that are understood and adhered to by all participants. Payment systems should support economies of scale while encouraging competition. Public and private regulators must also effectively oversee the payments network's stability and security, prevent fraud, and manage credit and financial risk concerns that threaten to undermine consumer confidence in new and existing electronic payments systems.

The Credit Card Industry Burdens Borrowers with Unfair Interest Rates and Hidden Fees

José García, James Lardner, and Cindy Zeldin

José García is associate director for Research Policy at Dēmos, a non-partisan public policy research and advocacy organization. He has written opinion articles for numerous newspapers and is the co-author of Up To Our Eyeballs: How Shady Lenders and Failed Economic Policies Are Drowning Americans in Debt, *from which this excerpt is taken. James Lardner is a journalist and senior fellow at Dēmos. Cindy Zeldin is federal affairs coordinator of the Economic Opportunity Program at Dēmos.*

Take an inventory of your wallet. If you find a few credit cards in there—or even a few more than a few—you can count yourself an average American of the early twenty-first century.[1] A credit card almost qualifies as a necessity nowadays. Try renting a car, booking an airplane trip, or engaging in almost any kind of online commerce without one.

In fact, convenience rather than credit is what many people are after when they apply for that first card. But circumstances change, and if you are like the majority of Americans, you have looked at your credit card statement in horror on at least a few occasions. Between 1989 and 2006, the nation's total credit card charges increased from about $69 billion a year to more than $1.8 trillion.[2] The proportion of households carrying a balance from month to month has grown (it was 58 percent in 2004), and the average amount owed by those house-holds has increased by a staggering 88 percent—from $2,768 in 1989 to $5,219 in 2004.[3]

Low- and Middle-Income Consumers Are Especially Vulnerable

In 2005, Demos and the Center for Responsible Lending com-missioned a survey of more than 1,100 middle- and low-income families with a recent history of unpaid balances. Nearly half the households in that survey reported having at least $5,000 in credit card debt; one-third owed $10,000 or more.[4]

A small fraction of these people traced their indebtedness back to spending on items that were neither critical nor nec-essary, such as a kitchen remodeling or the purchase of a ma-jor appliance. Far more pointed to basic living expenses such as rent and groceries, a medical or dental emergency, or a car repair. Many had started using credit cards in this way after a job loss. The survey results suggested a pattern in which one big blow—or one big burden—leaves resources so depleted that a family has to borrow for unusual and ordinary needs alike.

So let's say you owe a few thousand dollars or more. That, too, you may rest assured, is perfectly normal; and unless you are a very unusual borrower, you didn't run up your balance buying Manolo Blahnik shoes or Patek Philippe wristwatches. More likely, you slipped into debt while dealing with one of life's little financial emergencies. Then you found yourself us-ing credit cards to cover ordinary living expenses—gas, gro-ceries, utilities, rent—because it was the only way you knew how. . . .[5]

The Emergence of the Modern Credit Card

In the spring of 1990, three words sent convulsions through the credit card world. Those words—emblazoned across ads for a new AT&T credit card—were "No Annual Fee." AT&T's offer generated more than a quarter of a million responses on the first day, prompting other companies to bring out no-fee cards of their own.[16] Soon the $20 annual fees of the 1980s were history.[17] Eventually they would seem fairly benign, compared to what replaced them.

The modern credit card is really two products in one: a borrowing tool and a payment tool. With the disappearance of the annual fee, the cost burden shifted squarely onto the backs of the so-called revolvers—or serious borrowers—giving "convenience users," who routinely paid their bills in full, a free ride.[18] Unsurprisingly, one bank after another soon found that it had too few revolvers and too many convenience users (or, as some in the industry began calling them, "deadbeats"). To right the balance, lenders were tempted to go after people with shakier finances, since they were more likely to borrow; the only difficulty was that they would presumably also be more likely to default. Higher risk would mean higher interest rates at a time when they were already sky-high. In 1992, the industry average was 17.8 percent, about the same as it had been in 1980, even though the prime rate had meanwhile plunged from 13.4 to 3.5 percent. (In 2007, the average rate was 13.79 percent.)[19] The industry had already taken flak from consumer groups and elected officials for the widening spread between its own borrowing costs and those of its customers. Only a last-minute warning from the White House had kept Congress, in 1991, from passing a national usury law proposed by New York Republican senator Alfonse D'Amato.[20] Most lenders figured they were already charging as much as the market would bear.

Targeting a New Kind of Borrower

But most lenders were not as imaginative as a group of up-starts in San Francisco. Providian, as their company became known after a 1994 merger, had been founded (with backing from the Parker Pen Company) by Andrew Kahr. The company was shaped by Kahr's belief that the industry had focused on the wrong customer base—that is, on middle- and upper-middle-class people who would presumably make large purchases and be unlikely to default. Providian took a very different approach, going after customers that most credit card issuers wanted no part of. Divorced women, housewives who had never owned much of anything, people with sketchy or suspect credit records—Kahr and his colleagues believed there was gold in those unmined hills: vast numbers of customers who would eventually pay their debts, but who needed credit so badly that they would not look too closely at what it cost them. . . .[21]

Providian had been a pioneer in the marketing of so-called subprime credit cards. In the lending world, the word "prime" takes its meaning from the prime rate, which is the rate of interest charged by banks to the borrowers they consider most reliable. The prime sector of any lending market consists of the safest borrowers and situations; subprime means everything and everybody else. Since Kahr and his colleagues showed the way, subprime credit cards have become a huge industry.

Today, major banks as well as fringe players are involved, sometimes jointly. HSBC, the world's third-largest bank, owns Orchard Bank, a subprime company; it also has a refund anticipation loan (RAL) deal with H&R Block, the largest tax preparation company in the United States. Their RAL program provides taxpayers with short-term, fee-laden, triple-digit-interest loans that are secured by prospective tax refunds.[26] Capital One purveys the subprime EZN card in addition to its mainstream cards; some customers apply to Capital One expecting a normal card with a moderate interest rate, but wind up with a subprime card instead.[27]

The Subprime Market Yields Huge Profits

Before making headlines as the target of lawsuits and investigations, Providian gained the industry's attention with its financial performance. During the mid-1990s, the company enjoyed an average account balance of $4,500, while the industry norm was $1,800. It had a pretax profit margin of 5 percent, compared with an average of 3.2 percent, and its profits had grown by 20 percent a year or more for a decade.[28] It had achieved these results by, among other things, using low "introductory" interest rates to draw in customers; turning its credit limit into a revenue stream by approving "over the limit" purchases and charging extra for them; and lowering the minimum monthly payment to 2 percent of the balance—a level that could take up to half a century to pay off. All these techniques went on to become standard practice, not just in the subprime end of the market but across the spectrum of credit card issuers. (The only one that the industry has abandoned is the 2 percent minimum payment—and not by choice: in December 2005, federal bank regulators issued new rules that effectively raised the minimum payment to 4 percent.)[29]

> The prime sector of any lending market consists of the safest borrowers and situations; subprime means everything and everybody else.

In the early days of the credit card business, the cost of borrowing consisted largely of interest and the rate was clearly stated. In the new world that Kahr and his colleagues helped define, the official interest rate became just one among many charges, and not necessarily the most important one. . . .

The Supreme Court also deserves a share of the credit, though. Before the *Smiley* [*v. Citibank* 1996] decision on credit card fees, the typical credit card late fee was about $13. By 2005, it was nearly $34.[30] All told, late fees and over-the-limit fees generated $14.8 billion in revenue for the card companies in 2005.[31] Under the terms of many credit card contracts, late payments now also trigger a "penalty" or "default" interest rate; the average was 27 percent in 2005, with many issuers charging 30 percent or more.[36] Many credit card companies now start counting a payment as late if it comes after a certain time of day. (In one survey of card practices, only three banks—comparatively small ones—were found to not have penalty rates on their cards.)[37]

The tricks and traps that characterize the credit card business model generate robust profits, far greater than the profits derived from other areas of lending, largely because it is so woefully underregulated.

Banks Infringe on Borrowers' Rights

Many banks now assert the right to raise interest rates for reasons they need not specify in advance. Like Santa Claus, who "sees you when you're sleeping" and "knows when you're awake" credit card issuers are watching over their cardholders' financial conduct and making adjustments in response to things like a late or bounced payment to another creditor or even a casual inquiry about a potentially unwise loan.

In March 2007, Citibank renounced this practice, known as "universal default." Other banks, however, have stuck with it, and the broader enthusiasm for what [a professor of law at Harvard University and chair of the Congressional oversight panel for the government's Troubled Asset Relief Program] Elizabeth Warren calls "tricks and traps" continues unabated. All told, Americans now spend about $90 billion annually in interest and penalty payments on credit cards, or more than $800 per cardholding household. . . .[38]

Credit Card Services Squeeze Retailers Too

The credit card industry has often been accused of collusive pricing, and it's easy to see why such a suspicion might arise. In 1995, the top ten card issuers controlled slightly more than half the market; by 2006, their share was closing in on 90 percent. Two organizations, Visa and MasterCard, together account for about 80 percent of the transaction-processing end of the business. While their client banks control other pricing decisions, Visa and MasterCard themselves set the so-called interchange fees, the service charges paid by merchants. Retailer organizations have complained bitterly and repeatedly over these fees, which have doubled since 1995 despite technological advances that (merchants argue) should have made the credit card business more efficient. In 2005, interchange fees ranged between 1.6 and 1.7 percent, generating more than $30 billion in revenue.[41]

Long the most profitable area of banking, credit cards enjoy a return on assets more than three times that of commercial banking in general. In 2006, the industry earned an estimated $36.8 billion in profits, up nearly 80 percent from its 2000 level.[42] For example, according to Citigroup's SEC [Security and Exchange Commission] filings, the company's consumer lending business—encompassing such things as home mortgages, auto loans, and student loans—had a return on assets, or net profit, of 0.79 percent. The return on Citigroup's credit card lending business that year was 6.17 percent![43] The tricks and traps that characterize the credit card business model generate robust profits, far greater than the profits derived from other areas of lending, largely because it is so woefully underregulated.

While price-fixing may be a worry, it is not the only one. Over the past twenty-five years, the typical credit card agreement has expanded from one page to more than thirty pages, with the contract language often spread over multiple documents and not easily distinguished from reams of other verbiage.[44] Most agreements are written at a tenth- to twelfth-grade reading level, although half the population reads at or below an eighth-grade level.[45] Indeed, it is debatable whether any level of reading comprehension qualifies someone to wade through the thicket of fees, penalties, contingent interest rates, and legalisms of these contracts.

In 2006, credit card offers—including "preapproved" applications—added up to an estimated 8 billion pieces of direct mail.

Most Borrowers Do Not Consider Long-Term Ramifications

Can there really be such a thing as a free market or an informed consumer in a situation like this? A number of people who have studied the workings of the credit card industry have concluded that there can't be. Credit cards belong to a class of extremely complex pricing scenarios, [New York University Associate Professor of Law] Oren Bar-Gill argued in his 2004 monograph, "Seduction by Plastic," where a sophisticated seller will almost invariably get the better of an individual buyer.[46] In the lending field, this general problem may be compounded by the habitual tendency of borrowers to underestimate future, as opposed to present, financial difficulties. This "optimism bias," as some have termed it, produces decisions based on the up-front and obvious costs, as opposed to those that arise later and depend on certain contingencies of borrower behavior. Credit card companies routinely take advantage of the optimism bias, [University of Texas law professor] Ronald J. Mann writes in his book *Charging Ahead: The Growth and Regulation of Payment Card Markets*. They "identify a myopic class of customers and exploit the lack of rationality by systematically backloading the less attractive terms into a less prominent time and place in the relationship."[47]

Bar-Gill points out that "instead of bringing down interest rates and eliminating late and over-the-limit fees, competition is focused only on short-term perks." Consumers are encouraged to ignore the most dangerous costs—the ones that hit them when they are most vulnerable.[48] Competition can lead the managers of some companies to adopt practices that have improved the balance sheets of others, even if they never would have thought of those practices on their own. In other words, competition, far from being the solution, is part of the problem.

Since 1970, it has been illegal to send credit cards to people who have not requested them. But while that law may have cut down slightly on the amount of plastic that people receive in the mail, the volume of paper churned out by the industry has kept right on growing. In 2006, credit card offers—including "preapproved" applications—added up to an estimated 8 billion pieces of direct mail.[49]

No industry pushes its product harder, and these days it is difficult to find any sign of the old skittishness about fraud and default. In February 2007, Bank of America announced plans to issue a credit card designed expressly for undocumented aliens.[50] (It has yet to move forward with that plan, possibly because of some uneasiness expressed by immigration officials.) With "risk-based pricing," virtually all Americans are now seen as potential cardholders. But if the industry has singled out any one group for the greatest attention, it is the young—college students in particular.

Students Represent a Lucrative New Market for Issuers

Many Americans have their first encounter with the lending industry at freshman orientation, where credit card sales operatives can be found stationed at booths and tables, handing out Frisbees, T-shirts, and other goodies along with their application forms. Chase, in one recent year, offered free pedicab rides to any University of Michigan student willing to listen to an advertisement while cruising around the town of Ann Arbor.[51] The first visit to the campus bookstore becomes another opportunity to sign up for a card. Even more solicitations can be found pinned to bulletin boards or on popular Web sites like *Facebook.com*.[52]

Colleges and universities are in part to blame for the presence and prevalence of lenders on college campuses. Lenders are spending millions of dollars each year in contracts with colleges and universities to set up shop on campuses and solicit the highly profitable youth market.[53] In 2000, for example, First USA Bank (now Bank One) struck a $16.5 million deal with the University of Tennessee in Knoxville in exchange for contact information for students, associates, and alumni.[54] First USA had similar deals in as many as two hundred schools nationwide in 2002.[55]

For the credit card companies, the investment has paid off nicely. According to a study by [nonprofit student loan provider] Nellie Mae, three-quarters of all undergraduates use credit cards for school supplies (paper, notebooks, etc.), and nearly as many use them for textbooks. One in four students use their cards to help pay for tuition.[56] Gone are the days when minors had to get their parents to cosign a credit card application. In fact, savvy lenders would rather not have adults know too much; students make more use of their cards, the industry has found, when their parents are kept in the dark. According to the same survey, more than 90 percent of college seniors have at least one credit card, and many don't stop at one.[57] In 2004, the average senior had five cards and carried an average balance of $2,864. Almost one-quarter of students had credit card debt greater than $3,000.

The marketing of credit cards on college campuses has become a sensitive topic in Washington, with legislators frequently hinting at a crackdown. Meanwhile, the industry has pressed forward with efforts to reach an even younger demographic. In 2000, Visa began marketing a prepaid debit card called the Visa Buxx, "specially designed to offer teens spending independence and responsibility, while keeping parents informed, involved and in control."[58] Not to be outdone, MasterCard pitched its Hello Kitty debit card to high school and even junior high students.[59] (Pre-paid debit cards have been viewed by some in the industry as a way to get teenagers adjusted to using credit cards.) "We think our target age group will be from 10 to 14, although it could certainly go younger," said Bruce Giuliano, senior vice president of licensing for Sanrio Inc., which owns the Hello Kitty brand.[60]

Notes

1. Nilson Report, "Credit Cards—Holders, Numbers, Spending, and Debt," reported in *1998 Statistical Abstract of the United States* (Washington, DC: U.S. Government Printing Office, 1999), p. 523, table 822.

2. U.S. Government Accountability Office (GAO), *Credit Cards: Increased Complexity in Rates and Fees Heightens Need for More Effective Disclosures to Consumers*, Report to the Ranking Minority Member, Permanent Subcommittee on Investigations, Committee on Homeland Security and Governmental Affairs, U.S. Senate, GAO-06-929, September 2006, p. 1, http://www.gao.gov/; José García, *Borrowing to Make Ends Meet: National Statistics and Trends in Credit Card Debt, 2007 Update*, Demos, 2007.

3. José García, *Borrowing to Make Ends Meet; National Statistics and Trends in Credit Card Debt by Race and Age, 2007 Update*, Demos, 2007.

4. Demos and the Center for Responsible Lending, *The Plastic Safety Net: The Reality Behind Debt in America*, 2005, p. 7.

5. Ibid., p. 1.

16. Ibid. [Robin Stein, "Ascendancy of the Credit-Card Industry," *Frontline: Secret History of the Credit Card*, November 23, 2004.]; Jerry Hines, "Delight Makes the Difference: The Story of the AT&T Universal Card," *TQM Magazine 7*, no. 3 (1995), pp. 6–11; Dennis W. Carlton and Alan S. Frankel, "The Antitrust Economics of Credit Card Networks," *Antitrust Law Journal* 63, no. 2 (1995), p. 643.

17. Stein, "Ascendancy of the Credit Card Industry."

18. Ibid.

19. Cardweb.com, "Card Rates," March 19, 2007, http://www.cardweb.com/cardtrak/news/2007/march/19a.html.

20. Stein, "Ascendancy of the Credit Card Industry."

21. Saul Hansell, "Merchants of Debt," *New York Times*, July 2, 1995; Anne M. Petersen, "Lawsuits and Complaints Dog Credit Card Provider," Associated Press, June 1, 1999.

26. National Consumer Law Center and Consumer Federation, *Tax Preparers Peddle High-Priced Tax Refund Loans: Millions Skimmed from the Working Poor and the U.S. Treasury*, January 2002.

27. U.S. Senate Committee on Banking, Housing, and Urban Affairs, "Examining the Billing, Marketing, and Disclosure Practices of the Credit Card Industry," testimony of Robert D. Manning, January 25, 2007.

28. Ibid.

29. Mark Huffman, "Minimum Credit Card Payments Going Up, But How Much?" Consumer Affairs, December 19, 2005, http://www.consumeraffairs.com.

30. GAO, *Credit Cards*.

31. Cardweb.com, "Free Party," January 13, 2005, http://www.cardweb.com/cardtrak/news/2005/january/131.html.

36. GAO, *Credit Cards*, p. 24.

37. Consumer Action, "Credit Card Survey 2007," Spring 2007, http://www.consumer-action.org.

38. Gordon and Douglas, "Taking Charge." [Robert Gordon and Derek Douglas, "Taking Charge: Attention Credit-Card Companies: When We Want You to Charge Us Hidden Fees, We'll Let You Know," *Washington Monthly*, December 1, 2005.]

41. See UnfairCreditCardFees.com; Charles Lee, "Corporate Thievery," *University of Virginia Cavalier Daily*, January 22, 2007.

42. U.S. Senate Committee on Banking, Housing, and Urban Affairs, "Examining the Billing, Marketing, and Disclosure Practices of the Credit Card Industry," testimony of Travis Plunkett, January 25, 2007; Ellen Cannon, "Credit Card Issuers' Profits Grew," Bankrate.com, January 9, 2007, http://www.bankrate.com.

43. Citigroup 2006 SEC Filings, Form 10-K, pp. 22, 26, http://www.citigroup.com/citigroup/rm/data/k06c.pdf.

44. U.S. Senate Committee on Banking, Housing, and Urban Affairs, "Examining the Billing, Marketing, and Disclosure Practices of the Credit Card, Industry," testimony of Elizabeth Warren, January 25, 2007, p. 4.

45. GAO, *Credit Cards*, p. 6.

46. Oren Bar-Gill, "Seduction by Plastic," *Northwestern University Law Review* 98, no. 4 (2004), pp. 1373–434.

47. Ronald J. Mann, *Charging Ahead: The Growth and Regulation of Payment Card Markets* (New York: Cambridge University Press, 2006).

48. Bar-Gill, "Seduction by Plastic."

49. Cardweb.com, "Orvis Card," January 21, 2007, http:// www.cardweb.com/cardtrak/news/2007/february/21a.html.

50. Miriam Jordan, "Bank of America Casts Wider Net for Hispanics," *Wall Street Journal*, February 13, 2007.

51. Aaron Johnson, "Chase Hocks Credit Cards with Help of Bike Cabs," BankNet 360, October 23, 2006, http:// www.banknet360.com/.

52. Ibid.

53. Robert Manning, "Credit Cards on Campus," New American Dream, n.d., http://www.newdream.org/ newsletter/creditcards.php.

54. Ray Brady, "Students Hooked on Credit," CBS News, May 3, 2000.

55. Taylor Loyal, "Don't Leave Home Without It," *Mother Jones*, March/April 2002.

56. Nellie Mae Corporation, "Undergraduate Students and Credit Cards: An Analysis of Usage Rates and Trends," May 2005, http://www.nelliemae.com/pdf/ccstudy_2005.pdf.

57. Ibid.

58. Visa Buxx announcement, http://usa.visa.com/personal/ cards/prepaid/visa_buxx.html.

59. Caroline E. Mayer, "Girls Go from Hello Kitty to Hello Debit Card: Brand's Power Tapped to Reach Youth," *Washington Post*, October 3, 2004.

60. Ibid.

Credit Card Debt Disproportionately Affects Low- and Middle-Income Americans

Christian E. Weller

Christian E. Weller is a senior economist at the Center for American Progress, a progressive think tank in Washington, D.C., dedicated to improving the lives of Americans through ideas and action.

During the past few years, the United States has experienced an unprecedented boom in household debt. For the first time on record, families have outstanding debt that is greater than their incomes. To a large degree, this rise in debt is a consequence of rapidly rising costs for large ticket items such as housing, medical care, and education, amid flat or declining incomes.

Although most household debt is in the form of mortgages and home equity lines, credit card debt often receives particular attention. This is usually due to the costs associated with credit cards rather than because of the amount owed on credit cards. Credit card debt, of course, tends to carry high interest rates, large fees, and a number of hidden costs. These factors disproportionately affect lower income families, who are disproportionately renters, and thus, cannot borrow funds against their homes via home equity lines of credit, which is a significantly less costly form of debt.

Christian E. Weller, "Pushing the Limit: Credit Card Debt Burdens American Families," Center for American Progress, July 19, 2006, pp. 1–11. This material was created by the Center for American Progress www.americanprogress.org. Reproduced by permission.

Credit Card Debt Is on the Rise

A closer look at credit card debt shows the following:

- Credit card debt has become more widespread. A larger share of families (46.2 percent in 2004) than ever before carried credit card balances, up from 39.6 percent in 1989. Typical credit card debt has grown to its highest level on record. By 2004, the typical family with credit card debt owed $2,150 (in 2004 dollars), up 62.9 percent since 1989.

- Credit card debt levels relative to income are highest among low-income families. Low-income families owed the equivalent of 9.5 percent of their income on credit cards, while middle-class families owed 5.2 percent, and high-income families owed 2.3 percent.

- Typical credit card payments pose a small but disproportionate burden on families' incomes. Typical credit card payments relative to income rose faster than total payments from 1989 to 2004.

- Credit card debt contributes to families' financial struggles. The share of families with high credit card payments—above 10 percent of income—rose from 13.5 percent in 1989 to 23.0 percent in 2004.

- Delinquency rates are greater for families with high levels of credit card debt than for families with high levels of overall debt. While 9.9 percent of families with high credit card debt were 60 days late on at least one payment, 7.5 percent of families with high overall debt were 60 days late on at least one payment.

Credit Card Debt Particularly Impacts Low- and Moderate-Income Families

A number of regulatory changes have increased access to credit, especially in the form of mortgages and home equity lines. The standardization of mortgages and the introduction of mortgage-backed securities has reduced the costs of consumer debt. Changes in the tax code have also given rise to financial innovation, reducing the costs of particular forms of credit.

The Tax Reform Act of 1986, for example, phased out the deductibility of most non-mortgage interest and introduced new marginal tax rates that reduced the tax advantage of all types of debt, leading to a shift of consumer debt toward mortgages, including home equity lines. Many households, though, do not have access to these lower cost forms of credit, mainly because they do not own a home that they could offer as collateral.

Lower income families are caught in a bind. Their need to borrow in the face of falling incomes has gone up, but they only have access to more costly credit card debt.

Renters, though, tend to be disproportionately low-income families. Their incomes have grown slowly for much of the past decade, and have fallen more than for higher income families in recent years. Thus, lower income families are caught in a bind. Their need to borrow in the face of falling incomes has gone up, but they only have access to more costly credit card debt. This economic bind between the need to borrow and access to credit is reflected in a disproportionate share of credit card debt among low-income families.

Over time, the use of credit card debt has become more widespread, especially among low- and moderate-income families. The share of households with credit card debt among 20 percent of the lowest income families, for example, grew by 10.9 percentage points from 18.2 percent in 1989 to 29.2 percent in 2004, and it expanded by 9.5 percentage points from 34.7 percent to 44.2 percent for families on the next 20 percent rung of the income ladder.

During the same period, the share of families with credit card debt among all other families expanded much slower or even declined. Between 1989 and 2004, the share of families with credit card debt also grew faster among non-union families, minority families, young families, single women, and families with a high school education.

Credit Card Debt Reaches Record High Levels

Not only has the share of families with credit card debt increased, but also the typical amount of credit card debt. In 2004, the last year for which data are available, the outstanding credit card debt for the typical family was $2,150 (in 2004 dollars), an increase of 6.2 percent more than the level in 2001 and 62.9 percent greater than in 1989, the first year for which data are available.

The absolute amounts of credit card debt have expanded especially for middle- and moderate-income families. For instance, from 2001 to 2004, the amount of credit card debt grew by 40.8 percent for the 20 percent of families with incomes above those families at the bottom of the income scale. Among families with incomes in the middle 20 percent, credit card debt grew by 3.3 percent, and by 19.3 percent for the 20 percent of families just below those at the top of the income scale.

In comparison, credit card debt declined by 6.1 percent from 2001 to 2004 for the typical family among the 20 percent of families at the bottom of the income scale. This is the case even though credit card debt levels relative to income are highest among low income families.

Many demographic groups saw record high levels of credit card debt. This was true for middle-income families, for non-union households, for white and Hispanic families, for families with a high school education, and for those with at least a college degree. The picture, though, changes when credit card debt is set in relation to family income. Now, the relevance of credit card debt declines with credit. In line with the observation that lower income families may have the largest need to borrow on credit cards, the ratio of credit card debt to income rose fastest from 1989 to 2004 for low-income families and actually declined for high-income families.

Yet, there seems to be a limit as to how quickly low- and moderate-income families can expand their credit card debt relative to income. From 2001 to 2004, credit card debt relative to income fell for the 40 percent of families with the lowest incomes. While families at the bottom may have had the greatest need to borrow, they may have also experienced restricted access to credit card borrowing.

Credit Card Payments Rise Faster Than Payments for Other Forms of Credit

To see if credit card debt places a measurable burden on some families, three different measures are used: (1) the payments on credit card debt relative to income; (2) the share of families with disproportionately high levels of credit card debt payments; and (3) the share of families with delinquencies. In each case, the three metrics are calculated for families with low, typical, and high levels of credit card debt relative to income. These three groups are defined, so that there is the same number of people with any amount of credit card debt for each in any given year.

Debt payments relative to income have grown substantially between 1989 and 2004, albeit at comparatively low levels. During this 15-year period, the typical payment relative to income grew from 0.5 percent to 0.8 percent—an increase of 0.3 percentage points or 60.0 percent. At the same time, credit card debt levels relative to income increased by 58.1 percent, or 1.8 percentage points, from 3.1 percent in 1989 to 4.9 percent in 2004. That is, payments rose somewhat in proportion with debt levels.

Yet, when credit card payments are compared to total debt payments, their increase is disproportionate. While credit card payments relative to income grew by 60.0 percent, total debt payments relative to income rose from 16.3 percent in 1989 to 18.3 percent in 2004, an increase of only 12.2 percent.

This discrepancy is even more telling about the underlying costs of credit card debt—considering that credit card debt relative to income rose by 58 percent, and that total debt relative to income grew by 107.3 percent, from 52.3 percent in 1989 to 108.4 percent, in 2004. One possible explanation is that even though overall debt levels rose sharply the costs of those debts—interest rates—declined simultaneously, offsetting the rise in debt amounts. That is, with smaller increases in debt levels for credit cards than for total debt, credit card costs rose faster than total debt, highlighting the disproportionately higher costs of credit cards.

When credit card payments are compared to total debt payments, their increase is disproportionate.

The Share of Households with High Credit Card Payments Grows Sharply

The high cost of credit card debt also becomes apparent when considering the situation for the one-third of families with the highest credit card debt levels relative to income. For these families, the typical credit card payment was 1.7 percent of income in 1989, or more than three times as much as for the one-third of families with typical credit card levels. By 2004, the debt payments for families with high credit card debt rose to 3.2 percent of income, or four times the payments level for families with typical credit card debt. In comparison, the ratio of total debt payments for families with high debt levels and for those with typical debt levels was less than twice as much in both years.

Admittedly, credit card debt plays a comparatively small role for the typical family, even though it appears to carry a disproportionate burden. This is not to say that some families don't struggle under the yoke of heavy credit card interest rates and credit card fees. Case in point: 23 percent of families with high credit card levels paid more than 40 percent of their income for debt service—interest payments and principal in 2004, up from 13.5 percent in 1989. Also, 9.6 percent of families with high credit card debt paid more than 10 percent of their income to repay their credit card debt in 2004—the highest share during the 15-year period, for which data exist.

The growth rate from 2001 to 2004 alone was 50 percent, from 6.4 percent of income to 9.6 percent. At the same time, the share of heavily indebted families, or families with debt payments of 40 percent of income, grew much slower among families with high levels of debt, or by only 6.4 percent from 29.6 percent in 2001 to 31.5 percent in 2004. Again, credit card debt appears to contribute disproportionately to the struggles of families with debt.

Delinquencies Are on the Rise for Households with High Credit Card Debt

Another indication that credit card debt may play a disproportionate role in households' financial struggles is the link between credit card debt and the share of families who are delinquent on paying at least one bill. For instance, 9.9 percent of families with high credit card levels reported that they were 60 days late on at least one bill in 2004, as compared to 7.5 percent of families with high overall debt levels—a difference of 32 percent.

More importantly, this difference has widened over time. In 1989, 6.3 percent of families with credit card debt were delinquent on at least one bill, or 26 percent more than the 5.0 percent of families with high total debt.

Although credit card debt is a relatively small part of the credit boom that has characterized the U.S. economy for the past few years, it can impose a disproportionate burden on many families, particularly for low- and moderate-income families. Because they are often not home owners, they have only access to more costly forms of credit, such as credit cards. The data show that families with high credit card levels, which are disproportionately lower income, have indeed seen a disproportionate increase in credit card payments, heavy indebtedness, and delinquency rates from 1989 to 2004.

Stricter Lending Standards Force Credit Card Users to Modify Spending Habits

Daniel Gross

Daniel Gross is the Moneybox *columnist for* Slate *and the business columnist for* Newsweek. *He also is the author of* Dumb Money: How Our Greatest Financial Minds Bankrupted the Nation.

The most revolutionary notion in commerce today is one of the oldest. If you want to buy something, you may actually have to pay for it. We are reverting from a "borrow and buy" economy to the "cash and carry" model of our grandparents.

The Olesons may have extended store credit to Ma and Pa Ingalls in *Little House on the Prairie*, but widespread consumer credit is a very recent phenomenon. It began in the 1920s, when expensive consumer durables—cars, refrigerators—were first produced in mass quantities. It wasn't until Bank of America began carpet-bombing California with credit-card applications in the 1960s that the debt wave started in earnest.

In the decades since, consumer credit became so pervasive that paying cash became passé. Want a new $32,530 Dodge Ram Crew pickup? Take a lease. Sick of your old house? Get a 100 percent mortgage and trade up. Face lift? Round-the-world cruise? New PC? Three-hundred dollar sushi dinner at Nobu? Whip out that plastic. It was this behavior—the endless willingness of lenders to lend and borrowers to borrow—that kept the consumer economy humming uninterrupted from the early 1990s, straight through the brief recession of 2001, until the credit meltdown of 2007.

But many of the lenders who extended credit recklessly are now acting like a single twenty-something who, after having a few bad dates, takes a vow of celibacy. Students returning to college are finding that student loans have vanished. Retailers who freely extended credit to any customer with a pulse are deploying bean counters armed with sophisticated software to sniff out potential deadbeats. And when higher rates and fees don't deter their borrowers, credit-card companies resort to slashing credit lines. "We predicted there would be some degree of spillover from the mortgage meltdown," said Curtis Arnold, founder of *CardRatings.com*. "But the credit line reductions by big credit card companies in the last six months have been fairly unprecedented."

This shock to the system may further damage the already-fragile psychology of the consumer. Writing a check or deducting the price of a pair of shoes directly from your bank account packs a much more potent emotional punch than charging the pair of Allen Edmonds loafers on your American Express platinum card. Chalk it up to a concept called "the pain of paying," said Dan Ariely, the author of *Predictably Irrational*. (It's a concept the parents of his students at Duke University feel every semester.) Imagine that a restaurant, rather than charging $30 per meal, charged 50 cents per bite, with a waiter standing tableside collecting after each chomp. That would be an extremely unpleasant meal. But credit puts a safe distance between the ecstasy of consumption and the agony of payment, and thus makes us feel better. Said Ariely: "If it's more difficult to get credit, it might make people feel more pain of paying and therefore spend less."

The availability of credit also changes the calculus people use to determine what they can afford. Blowing $6,000 on a week in Tuscany might be tough to swing if you have to pay for it all next month. Convince yourself it's a once-in-a-lifetime experience that you can pay for over three years, and it becomes a bargain. With credit, Saturday night means dinner and a movie. When you pay cash and have a fixed budget, it's dinner or a movie.

The lack of credit makes things seem more expensive to consumers, even if prices are holding steady.

The tightening of credit is forcing more people to confront these uncomfortable choices. In the second quarter, credit giant MasterCard reported that the gross dollar volume, or GDV, of credit charges processed in the United States rose just 0.7 percent from 2007, while the GDV of debit charges rose 15.8 percent. The huge retailer Target in late August said that in the second quarter, for the first time in memory, the percentage of sales charged to credit cards fell, while the proportion of purchases made with debit cards rose. That's partially by design, since the company has undertaken an "aggressive reduction of credit lines and significant tightening of all aspects of our underwriting." (Translation: No credit for you!!)

Leverage is an appropriate synonym for credit because it allows you to lift more than you could with simply your own financial muscle. Take away the leverage, and the power lifter becomes a 98-pound weakling. That's clearly a factor in the housing market. In 2007, according to the National Association of Realtors, 45 percent of first-time homebuyers put no money down, and the median first-time homebuyer financed a massive 98 percent of the purchase. But no-money-down mortgages, like Rudy Giuliani's presidential candidacy, began fading in late 2007 and largely disappeared in the cruel winter of 2008. No wonder existing home sales fell 13.2 percent in July from last year while new home sales plummeted 35.3 percent.

In effect, the lack of credit makes things seem more expensive to consumers, even if prices are holding steady. And in a world of scarce credit, consumption is likely to resemble a meal at Dan Ariely's nightmare restaurant: a series of small bites rather than an all-you-can-eat extravaganza.

The Dramatic Increase in National Credit Card Debt Could Devastate the Economy

Peter D. Schiff

Peter D. Schiff is an economic commentator, author, and licensed stockbroker. He is the author of Crash Proof: How to Profit from the Coming Economic Collapse *and* The Little Book of Bull Moves in Bear Markets: How to Keep Your Portfolio Up When the Market Is Down.

For those holding out hope [as of May 2008] that the American economy can miraculously avoid a long and deep recession, consumer credit is often viewed as the wonder drug that can cure all manner of economic ills. As such, last week's report showing that consumer credit grew by $15 billion was widely heralded as proof of America's economic strength and resilience.

The reality is very different, however: We're already suffering from the after-effects of too much debt, meaning that our salvation cannot be found in more of the same.

Credit Card Debt Is Becoming Impossible to Pay Down

Credit card debt, which now stands at whopping $957 billion nationally (approximately $3,000 for every U.S. citizen) has, in recent years, taken on a different role in the life of American consumers.

In the past, credit cards were used primarily to purchase big-ticket items, enabling consumers to spread the costs out over many months, making goods a bit more affordable.

Now, however, charge cards are increasingly being used to bridge the gap between cost of living and the diminishing purchasing power of Americans who have been taxed mercilessly by inflation. By buying with available credit instead of unavailable cash, consumers are not simply postponing the pain of higher prices, but compounding it by packing interest expenses into the costs of everyday purchases. In addition, as home equity credit is now unavailable to fund large purchases, many consumers are turning to non-deductible, higher-cost credit card debt as their last remaining lifeline. As such, credit card debt compounds steadily, and for many borrowers, becomes increasingly impossible to pay down.

The statistics tell the tale. According to Equifax Inc. (EFX), a credit card analysis firm, people have been buying more with their credit cards but paying down less. As a result, average balances jumped nearly 9% in 2007 and delinquency rates recently hit a four-year high of 4.5%.

By going even deeper into debt just to make ends meet, American consumers are digging themselves, and our entire economy, into an ever-deeper economic hole and laying the foundation for the next major credit debacle.

Expanded Consumer Credit Weakens the Economy

Also, the reliance on credit cards is preventing some of the market's salutary forces from working. With credit always an option, domestic demand remains strong—despite rising prices. Absent the option of putting more costly gasoline on their credit cards, Americans might have actually been forced to cut back on their fuel consumption, taking some of the upward pressure off gas prices.

It should be painfully obvious that expanded consumer credit is actually evidence of deterioration—not improvement.

Unfortunately, when it comes to understanding the economy, there is little common sense on display. By going even deeper into debt just to make ends meet, American consumers are digging themselves, and our entire economy, into an ever-deeper economic hole and laying the foundation for the next major credit debacle. It's fitting that just as both U.S. Treasury Secretary Henry M. Paulson and JP Morgan Chase & Co. (JPM) Chief Executive Officer Jamie Dimon declared that the worst of the crisis has past, we are on the verge of kicking this credit mess into a much-higher gear.

My guess is that many Americans continue to run up massive credit card debt because they have little intention of ever paying it off. Since many who are underwater on their home loans, and behind on their auto and student loans, too, see bankruptcy as a foregone conclusion, they see no reason not to just go ahead and pile on as much debt as possible while the taps remain open.

Hoping for a Government Bailout

Those choking off credit-card debt may also be taking cheer from the gathering government campaign to bail out over-leveraged homeowners. The sheer numbers of consumers who are afflicted with spiraling monthly payments will make credit card relief a potent political issue for crusading congressional and presidential candidates. After all, there are few fundamental differences between those who borrowed too much to buy houses and those who made the same mistake with consumer goods.

If the government bails out the former, then why not the latter, as well? In fact, one reason some homeowners have such large mortgages is that they consolidated their credit card debts into their mortgages each time they refinanced. Why should renters be forced to pay off their credit card debts while homeowners get to have their debts forgiven?

It's certainly a fair question.

But it may also be moot. Soon, as credit-card delinquencies rise—and losses on pools of securitized credit card debt mount—those supplying the credit will finally get wise to the fact they will never get their money back. As a result, the market for such debt will dry up even more quickly than did the market for subprime mortgages. Credit cards will therefore be much harder to come by and will have much lower limits then they do today. Limited to only the cash in their wallets, Americans finally will be forced to dramatically curtail their spending, and the recession will finally gather serious momentum.

Do Lenders and Debt Collection Agencies Treat Borrowers Fairly?

Overview: Paying Off Consumer Debt

Federal Trade Commission

The Federal Trade Commission (FTC) is a U.S. government agency that promotes consumer protection and monitors competition and financial practices in the economic sector.

Having trouble paying your bills? Getting dunning notices from creditors? Are your accounts being turned over to debt collectors? Are you worried about losing your home or your car?

You're not alone. Many people face a financial crisis some time in their lives. Whether the crisis is caused by personal or family illness, the loss of a job, or overspending, it can seem overwhelming. But often, it can be overcome. Your financial situation doesn't have to go from bad to worse.

If you or someone you know is in financial hot water, consider these options: realistic budgeting, credit counseling from a reputable organization, debt consolidation, or bankruptcy. Debt negotiation is yet another option. How do you know which will work best for you? It depends on your level of debt, your level of discipline, and your prospects for the future.

Writing down all your expenses, even those that seem insignificant, is a helpful way to track your spending patterns, identify necessary expenses, and prioritize the rest.

Planning Is Better Than Procrastination

Developing a Budget: The first step toward taking control of your financial situation is to do a realistic assessment of how much money you take in and how much money you spend.

Federal Trade Commission, "Knee Deep in Debt," FTC Facts for Consumers, 2005, pp. 1–6.

Start by listing your income from all sources. Then, list your "fixed" expenses—those that are the same each month—like mortgage payments or rent, car payments, and insurance premiums. Next, list the expenses that vary—like entertainment, recreation, and clothing. Writing down all your expenses, even those that seem insignificant, is a helpful way to track your spending patterns, identify necessary expenses, and prioritize the rest. The goal is to make sure you can make ends meet on the basics: housing, food, health care, insurance, and education.

Your public library and bookstores have information about budgeting and money management techniques. In addition, computer software programs can be useful tools for developing and maintaining a budget, balancing your checkbook, and creating plans to save money and pay down your debt.

Contacting Your Creditors: Contact your creditors immediately if you're having trouble making ends meet. Tell them why it's difficult for you, and try to work out a modified payment plan that reduces your payments to a more manageable level. Don't wait until your accounts have been turned over to a debt collector. At that point, your creditors have given up on you.

Dealing with Debt Collectors: The Fair Debt Collection Practices Act is the federal law that dictates how and when a debt collector may contact you. A debt collector may not call you before 8 a.m., after 9 p.m., or while you're at work if the collector knows that your employer doesn't approve of the calls. Collectors may not harass you, lie, or use unfair practices when they try to collect a debt. And they must honor a written request from you to stop further contact.

Act Quickly to Protect Your Home and Car

Managing Your Auto and Home Loans: Your debts can be unsecured or secured. Secured debts usually are tied to an asset, like your car for a car loan, or your house for a mortgage. If you stop making payments, lenders can repossess your car or foreclose on your house. Unsecured debts are not tied to any asset, and include most credit card debt, bills for medical care, signature loans, and debts for other types of services.

Most automobile financing agreements allow a creditor to repossess your car any time you're in default. No notice is required. If your car is repossessed, you may have to pay the balance due on the loan, as well as towing and storage costs, to get it back. If you can't do this, the creditor may sell the car. If you see default approaching, you may be better off selling the car yourself and paying off the debt: You'll avoid the added costs of repossession and a negative entry on your credit report.

If you fall behind on your mortgage, contact your lender immediately to avoid foreclosure. Most lenders are willing to work with you if they believe you're acting in good faith and the situation is temporary. Some lenders may reduce or suspend your payments for a short time. When you resume regular payments, though, you may have to pay an additional amount toward the past due total. Other lenders may agree to change the terms of the mortgage by extending the repayment period to reduce the monthly debt. Ask whether additional fees would be assessed for these changes, and calculate how much they total in the long term.

If you and your lender cannot work out a plan, contact a housing counseling agency. Some agencies limit their counseling services to homeowners with FHA [Federal Housing Administration] mortgages, but many offer free help to any homeowner who's having trouble making mortgage payments. Call the local office of the Department of Housing and Urban Development or the housing authority in your state, city, or county for help in finding a legitimate housing counseling agency near you.

Organizations Can Help Solve Financial Problems

Credit Counseling: If you're not disciplined enough to create a workable budget and stick to it, can't work out a repayment plan with your creditors, or can't keep track of mounting bills, consider contacting a credit counseling organization. Many credit counseling organizations are nonprofit and work with you to solve your financial problems. But be aware that, just because an organization says it's "nonprofit," there's no guarantee that its services are free, affordable, or even legitimate. In fact, some credit counseling organizations charge high fees, which may be hidden, or urge consumers to make "voluntary" contributions that can cause more debt.

Most credit counselors offer services through local offices, the Internet, or on the telephone. If possible, find an organization that offers in-person counseling. Many universities, military bases, credit unions, housing authorities, and branches of the U.S. Cooperative Extension Service operate nonprofit credit counseling programs. Your financial institution, local consumer protection agency, and friends and family also may be good sources of information and referrals.

Be aware that, just because an organization says it's "nonprofit," there's no guarantee that its services are free, affordable, or even legitimate.

Reputable credit counseling organizations can advise you on managing your money and debts, help you develop a budget, and offer free educational materials and workshops. Their counselors are certified and trained in the areas of consumer credit, money and debt management, and budgeting. Counselors discuss your entire financial situation with you, and help you develop a personalized plan to solve your money problems. An initial counseling session typically lasts an hour, with an offer of follow-up sessions.

Debt Management Plans Can Provide Structure

Debt Management Plans: If your financial problems stem from too much debt or your inability to repay your debts, a credit counseling agency may recommend that you enroll in a debt management plan (DMP). *A DMP alone is not credit counseling, and DMPs are not for everyone. You should sign up for one of these plans only after a certified credit counselor has spent time thoroughly reviewing your financial situation, and has offered you customized advice on managing your money.* Even if a DMP is appropriate for you, a reputable credit counseling organization still can help you create a budget and teach you money management skills.

In a DMP, you deposit money each month with the credit counseling organization, which uses your deposits to pay your unsecured debts, like your credit card bills, student loans, and medical bills, according to a payment schedule the counselor develops with you and your creditors. Your creditors may agree to lower your interest rates or waive certain fees, but check with all your creditors to be sure they offer the concessions that a credit counseling organization describes to you. A successful DMP requires you to make regular, timely payments, and could take 48 months or more to complete. Ask the credit counselor to estimate how long it will take for you to complete the plan. You may have to agree not to apply for—or use—any additional credit while you're participating in the plan.

Be wary of credit counseling organizations that:

- charge high up-front or monthly fees for enrolling in credit counseling or a DMP.

- pressure you to make "voluntary contributions," another name for fees.

- won't send you free information about the services they provide without requiring you to provide personal financial information, such as credit card account numbers, and balances.

- try to enroll you in a DMP without spending time reviewing your financial situation.

- offer to enroll you in a DMP without teaching you budgeting and money management skills.

- demand that you make payments into a DMP before your creditors have accepted you into the program.

Using Your Home as Collateral

You may be able to lower your cost of credit by consolidating your debt through a second mortgage or a home equity line of credit. Remember that these loans require you to put up your home as collateral. If you can't make the payments—or if your payments are late—you could lose your home.

What's more, the costs of consolidation loans can add up. In addition to interest on the loans, you may have to pay "points," with one point equal to one percent of the amount you borrow. Still, these loans may provide certain tax advantages that are not available with other kinds of credit.

A Debt Solution of Last Resort

Personal bankruptcy generally is considered the debt management option of last resort because the results are long-lasting and far reaching. People who follow the bankruptcy rules receive a discharge—a court order that says they don't have to repay certain debts. However, bankruptcy information (both the date of your filing and the later date of discharge) stays on your credit report for 10 years, and can make it difficult to obtain credit, buy a home, get life insurance, or sometimes get a job. Still, bankruptcy is a legal procedure that offers a fresh start for people who have gotten into financial difficulty and can't satisfy their debts.

There are two primary types of personal bankruptcy: Chapter 13 and Chapter 7. Each must be filed in federal bankruptcy court. As of April 2006, the filing fees run about $274 for Chapter 13 and $299 for Chapter 7. Attorney fees are additional and can vary.

Effective October 2005, Congress made sweeping changes to the bankruptcy laws. The net effect of these changes is to give consumers more incentive to seek bankruptcy relief under Chapter 13 rather than Chapter 7. Chapter 13 allows people with a steady income to keep property, like a mortgaged house or a car, that they might otherwise lose through the bankruptcy process. In Chapter 13, the court approves a repayment plan that allows you to use your future income to pay off your debts during a three-to-five-year period, rather than surrender any property. After you have made all the payments under the plan, you receive a discharge of your debts.

Bankruptcy information . . . stays on your credit report for 10 years, and can make it difficult to obtain credit, buy a home, get life insurance, or sometimes get a job.

Chapter 7 is known as straight bankruptcy, and involves liquidation of all assets that are not exempt. Exempt property may include automobiles, work-related tools, and basic household furnishings. Some of your property may be sold by a court-appointed official—a trustee—or turned over to your creditors. The new bankruptcy laws have changed the time period during which you can receive a discharge through Chapter 7. You now must wait 8 years after receiving a discharge in Chapter 7 before you can file again under that chapter. The Chapter 13 waiting period is much shorter and can be as little as two years between filings.

Borrowers Are Still Held Accountable

Both types of bankruptcy may get rid of unsecured debts and stop foreclosures, repossessions, garnishments and utility shut-offs, and debt collection activities. Both also provide exemptions that allow people to keep certain assets, although exemption amounts vary by state. Note that personal bankruptcy usually does not erase child support, alimony, fines, taxes, and some student loan obligations. And, unless you have an acceptable plan to catch up on your debt under Chapter 13, bankruptcy usually does not allow you to keep property when your creditor has an unpaid mortgage or security lien on it.

Another major change to the bankruptcy laws involves certain hurdles that a consumer must clear before even filing for bankruptcy, no matter what the chapter. You must get credit counseling from a government-approved organization within six months before you file for any bankruptcy relief. You can find a state-by-state list of government-approved organizations at *www.usdoj.gov/ust*. That is the website of the U.S. Trustee Program, the organization within the U.S. Department of Justice that supervises bankruptcy cases and trustees. Also, before you file a Chapter 7 bankruptcy case, you must satisfy a "means test." This test requires you to confirm that your income does not exceed a certain amount. The amount varies by state and is publicized by the U.S. Trustee Program at *www.usdoj.gov/ust*.

Debt Negotiation Is a Risky Proposition

Debt negotiation differs greatly from credit counseling and DMPs. It can be very risky, and have a long term negative impact on your credit report and, in turn, your ability to get credit. That's why many states have laws regulating debt negotiation companies and the services they offer. Contact your state Attorney General for more information.

The Claims. Debt negotiation firms may claim they're non-profit. They also may claim that they can arrange for your unsecured debt—typically credit card debt—to be paid off for anywhere from 10 to 50 percent of the balance owed. For example, if you owe $10,000 on a credit card, a debt negotiation firm may claim it can arrange for you to pay it off with a lesser amount, say $4,000.

The firms often pitch their services as an alternative to bankruptcy. They may claim that using their services will have little or no negative impact on your ability to get credit in the future, or that any negative information can be removed from your credit report when you complete their debt negotiation program. The firms usually tell you to stop making payments to your creditors, and instead, send payments to the debt negotiation company. The firm may promise to hold your funds in a special account and pay your creditors on your behalf.

The Truth. Just because a debt negotiation company describes itself as a "nonprofit" organization, there's no guarantee that the services they offer are legitimate. There also is no guarantee that a creditor will accept partial payment of a legitimate debt. In fact, if you stop making payments on a credit card, late fees and interest usually are added to the debt each month. If you exceed your credit limit, additional fees and charges also can be added. This can cause your original debt to double or triple. What's more, most debt negotiation companies charge consumers substantial fees for their services, including a fee to establish the account with the debt negotiator, a monthly service fee, and a final fee of a percentage of the money you've supposedly saved.

While creditors have no obligation to agree to negotiate the amount a consumer owes, they have a legal obligation to provide accurate information to the credit reporting agencies, including your failure to make monthly payments. That can result in a negative entry on your credit report. And in certain situations, creditors may have the right to sue you to recover the money you owe. In some instances, when creditors win a lawsuit, they have the right to garnish your wages or put a lien on your home. Finally, the Internal Revenue Service may consider any amount of forgiven debt to be taxable income.

Borrowers Should Do Homework When Considering Help for Debt

Turning to a business that offers help in solving debt problems may seem like a reasonable solution when your bills become unmanageable. But before you do business with any company, check it out with your state Attorney General, local consumer protection agency, and the Better Business Bureau. They can tell you if any consumer complaints are on file about the firm you're considering doing business with. Ask your state Attorney General if the company is required to be licensed to work in your state and, if so, whether it is.

Some businesses that offer to help you with your debt problems may charge high fees and fail to follow through on the services they sell. Others may misrepresent the terms of a debt consolidation loan, failing to explain certain costs or mention that you're signing over your home as collateral. Businesses advertising voluntary debt reorganization plans may not explain that the plan is a bankruptcy filing, tell you everything that's involved, or help you through what can be a long and complex process.

Only time and a conscientious effort to repay your debts will improve your credit report.

In addition, some companies guarantee you a loan if you pay a fee in advance. The fee may range from $100 to several hundred dollars. Resist the temptation to follow up on these advance-fee loan guarantees. They may be illegal. It is true that many legitimate creditors offer extensions of credit through telemarketing and require an application or appraisal fee in advance. But legitimate creditors never guarantee that the consumer will get the loan—or even represent that a loan is likely. Under the federal Telemarketing Sales Rule, a seller or tele-marketer who guarantees or represents a high likelihood of your getting a loan or some other extension of credit may not ask for or accept payment until you've received the loan.

You should be cautious of claims from so-called credit repair clinics. Many companies appeal to consumers with poor credit histories, promising to clean up credit reports for a fee. But you already have the right to have any inaccurate information in your file corrected. And a credit repair clinic cannot have accurate information removed from your credit report, despite their promises. You also should know that federal and some state laws prohibit these companies from charging you for their services until the services are fully performed. Only time and a conscientious effort to repay your debts will improve your credit report.

If you're thinking about getting help to stabilize your financial situation, do some homework first. Find out what services a business provides and what it costs, and don't rely on verbal promises. Get everything in writing, and read your contracts carefully.

The Best Way to Avoid Debt Collectors Is Not to Go into Debt

Llewellyn H. Rockwell Jr.

Llewellyn H. Rockwell Jr. is president of the Ludwig von Mises Institute, a research and educational center of classical liberalism, libertarian political theory, and the Austrian School of economics in Auburn, Alabama. He also is the editor of LewRockwell.com *and the author of* Speaking of Liberty.

You know hypocrisy, as when the pot calls the kettle black? Well, this news report gives new meaning to the idea:

> The rise in American consumer debt has been accompanied by a sharp increase in complaints about aggressive and sometimes unscrupulous tactics by debt collection agencies, a phenomenon that has government regulators increasingly concerned.

So the government is concerned about rough tactics, huh? Try skipping out on your taxes this year and see how rough the tactics can become. Try hiring an employee at less than the official wage floor and see what becomes of your business. Try to put a tool shed on the "wetland" in your backyard and see what the regulators do.

The Government Is Hypocritical About Aggressive Conduct

If foreign producers try selling too many peanuts or t-shirts, or attempt to charge a genuine market price, the whole weight of leviathan comes down on their heads. If their government

Llewellyn H. Rockwell Jr., "In Defense of Debt Collectors," *LewRockwell.com*, July 6, 2006. Reproduced by permission.

leaders say something nasty about the US president, they risk being overthrown or having their cities blown up.

In other words, the US government is in no position to complain about rough tactics in the seizure of property.

What's more, the government acts without prior contract. No one is ever asked if he would or would not like to pay taxes, obey regulations, or adhere to US dictates on trade or foreign policy. The government presumes that you are under its control just because you happen to be born within territory that it controls. In short, the government always and everywhere acts *aggressively*, which means to use force against someone without any basis in contract.

In contrast, the surest way to avoid being bugged by private debt collectors is not to go into debt. They will not and cannot take money from you that you otherwise have not promised to give them. If, however, you have promised to pay in the future, but received goods or services in the present, you owe and you must pay.

Sometimes people agree to pay, receive goods and services, and then refuse to pay. This is called stealing.

Sometimes people agree to pay, receive goods and services, and then refuse to pay. This is called stealing. The market economy discourages this through the critical institution called the credit rating. The credit rating is a measure of trust and character. It tells future lenders what kind of person you are, and whether you can be relied upon to live up to your obligations. These things do tend to follow patterns, after all.

In any case, the institution of the credit rating rewards people for keeping their commitments and punishes those who do not. It is a way in which the free market helps form good character and improve the culture—all without government design.

Debt Collectors Perform an Essential Service

So what happens to those who don't pay, i.e. steal? They have to give the property or its equivalent back. That is where the debt collectors come in. They are unpopular figures, to be sure. But they are essential.

And yes, they use forceful tactics, but let's be clear about the distinction between the aggression the government uses on an ongoing basis, which cannot be squared with morality, and the general use of force, which can be squared with morality provided it is used in defense of property and person.

Debt collection, then, is nothing but the use of retributive force in the defense of property—a wholly legitimate function of some agencies in a free society.

But leave it to the government—which claims the monopoly on the use of force—to make life hard for those who are using force for legitimate reasons.

The Federal Trade Commission is all ears when it comes to complaints about debt-collection agencies. They receive complaints all the time and then use muscle against people who are merely trying to recover stolen property.

Apparently, attempts to collect are intensifying since bankruptcy laws have been tightened. But if you care about the security of property, this is a positive trend.

Let the Industry Regulate Itself

Now, the story in question cites a number of cases when the credit collection agency apparently went after the wrong person and behaved imperviously to protests. This can happen, as in the case of identity theft or technical error. What happens in this case? Most such situations are eventually resolved through agreement. A collection agency that targets the wrong guy too often gets weeded out of the market. This is because no business has any long-term interest in trying to collect money that is not theirs.

You don't need government to step in as a police force to determine which agencies are good and accurate or bad and inaccurate. These systems can be internally self-policing. And contrary to the legend, no company wants to have to collect bad debts; indeed, it is very costly to do so. A credit-card company or car lot would far rather work out a deal than have to search and seize. There are no vast profits to be had in making people live up to their commitments.

Compare, too, what happens when a private agency makes a mistake to when the government makes a mistake. In private markets, the case can be frustrating and, yes, even humiliating. But there are open avenues to set the record straight. But when government has a case of mistaken identity, you can find yourself languishing in jail or even go to the electric chair. Government doesn't easily admit error, whereas private markets have the incentive to discover errors and fix them.

The repo man is one of the most unpopular people in society. But he serves an essential function of ensuring the protection of property, which is the foundation of freedom. When the government makes it difficult to collect debts, we need not be naïve about the real nature of what is going on. The government is only seeking to shore up its monopoly on the use of force, and make life difficult for those who want to use peaceful methods of drawing sharp distinctions between what is mine and what is thine.

Evangelical Financial Advisers Inspire Debtors to Regain Control of Their Finances

Jason Byassee

Jason Byassee is an assistant editor for Christian Century.

Heather from Oregon sounds like a born-again woman, financially speaking. "I finally got *everything* paid off this spring. . . . No more credit cards, no more student loan! I feel so good, so adult, and *so proud of myself.*" She thanks her deliverer, radio personality, and anticredit crusader Dave Ramsey, for freeing her from bondage to consumer debt, and he published her note at *daveramsey.com* as the testimony of another satisfied customer.

Ramsey is a tough-talking, quick-witted evangelical radio personality out of Nashville whose ability to offer paternalistic financial advice and to turn a phrase has earned him millions of listeners, both religions and secular. The Financial Peace University, a spinoff of his radio program, offers curricula for church groups. His 13-week seminar promises to help the average family reduce debt by $5,300 and save $2,700, according to the marketing materials on his Web site.

Those savings presumably make for more money in the church's offering plate. A spokesperson for Crown Financial Ministries, headquartered in Gainesville, Georgia, told the *Dallas Morning News* that graduates of Crown's small-group study increase their giving to the church by more than 60 percent. What church wouldn't pay the $289 study fee and ask for $89 from each participant in return for the sort of joy that gushes from Heather from Oregon, or from her pastor?

An Evangelical Approach to Finance

Ramsey's financial advice is tied to an evangelical Christian message. Scriptural teaching and practical advice go hand in hand. He quotes Paul, seemingly an unlikely source for financial wisdom: "Owe no one anything except to love one another" (Rom. 13:8). He constantly preaches against flashy consumerism: "Barbie and Ken (you know, the couple who *appear* to be perfect—perfect clothes, perfect car, perfect house) are broke, and I don't take financial advice from broke people anymore." Ramsey often tells the story of how he made and lost a fortune in real estate in his 20s before determining to learn how money really works. He told *Christianity Today* last year [2006] that "a whole bunch of us got all this stuff we really didn't want with money we really didn't have to impress people we really didn't like." Ramsey claims that 37 percent of marital problems stem from tension over finances.

Other evangelical groups, including the Good Sense Ministry at Willow Creek Community Church in Illinois, proffer similar kinds of advice. All offer a form of tough love when it comes to debt: debt, they say, is spiritually debilitating. It is likely that they would prefer to call it sin but have the pastoral sense not to blame people who are in the early stages of recovery. The way out of such bondage, they say, begins with setting up a basic budget. They instruct families to start their budget by allocating 10 percent to the church (pastors, don't reach for the phone yet) and 10 percent to savings. If the remaining 80 percent of income doesn't cover expenses, then something has to give: find another job, trade down in housing or sell off some assets.

These counselors' main message is that borrowing—some say even for a home, car or education—is bad. There is some variation on this point. Good Sense is not allergic to all kinds of debt; it merely discourages unsecured borrowing, in which the purchase can't be easily resold and the debt repaid, as with a car or house. Ramsey's and Crown's repudiation of debt is more sweeping, though a spokesperson at Crown insisted that its stance is not absolute. "Crown has never said that borrowing is prohibited in scripture," a spokesperson wrote me in an e-mail. But the e-mail message continued: "It is not recommended and never gives God glory."

Anyone who has struggled to master his or her finances rather than be mastered by them knows the profound relief that can come from setting one's house in order.

Financial Advice Can Be Found in the Bible

Crown provides an assemblage of biblical passages to describe the misery of indebtedness, such as Proverbs 22:7: "The borrower is servant to the lender." The passages come primarily from the wisdom tradition, though occasionally passages from the New Testament are also invoked, such as Luke 14:28, in which Jesus asks, "Which one of you, when he wants to build a tower, does not first sit down and calculate the cost to see if he has enough to complete it?" Crown comments, "You might have to go through a similar reasoning process regarding your home if your housing costs are too high for your income."

This way of reading the text ignores the broader context of the message: Jesus is talking about counting the cost of following the way of the cross. Crown turns Jesus' words into the sort of advice that could come from *Poor Richard's Almanac.* Its overall use of biblical material is legalistic—the Bible offers a set of rules to be followed in pursuit of certain reward. At its worst this can veer toward Pelagianism—the teaching, combated by St. Augustine, that views salvation as a reward for good works. The testimony of Heather from Oregon evinces the sort of joy that evangelicals once reserved for speaking of their conversion. Furthermore, and most problematically Jesus' more demanding teachings on the giving up of possessions are ignored entirely. Jesus himself seems surprisingly immaterial to these evangelical ministries.

But anyone who has struggled to master his or her finances rather than be mastered by them knows the profound relief that can come from setting one's house in order. And with the average U.S. household carrying between $10,000 and $15,000 in credit card debt (estimates vary), the problem these ministries have identified is real. Credit card debt has almost tripled since 1989, and consumer debt generally is over $1 trillion, perhaps approaching $2 trillion. Laws regulating the behavior of predatory lenders have been slashed, allowing credit card companies to raise their annual interest rates to preposterous levels—30 percent or more—and to raise them at any time, for any reason.

Card companies make the bulk of their profit from consumers who carry a balance from month to month, accruing high interest. Elizabeth Warren, who teaches bankruptcy law at Harvard, says card companies derisively refer to those who pay their bills on time as "deadbeats." Patently usurious "payday" lending stores continue to mushroom, despite the critical media attention they have received. The disastrous effect of subprime lending on the real estate market has been widely noted.

Card companies derisively refer to those who pay their bills on time as "deadbeats."

Christian Financial Planners Give Debtors Hope

It is no wonder that many people, and not only Christians, are tuning in to what these Christian financial advisers are saying. Some 200,000 people "graduated" from Ramsey's Financial Peace University last year. His radio show is carried on hundreds of nonreligious stations, and plans are being made for a televised version of Ramsey's show with CBS/Paramount. Crown's many radio programs reach 1 million listeners, and its Web site boasts of plans to reach 300 million people by 2015. Crown bills itself as "the world's largest Christian financial ministry." Good Sense offers more modest numbers, claiming that its resources are used by some 4,000 churches.

Many of these clients and listeners are members of mainline churches. According to the *United Methodist Reporter*, some 900 UMC [United Methodist Church] churches are using materials from Financial Peace University. Crown reports that some 20 percent of its subscribers are mainline Protestants (interestingly, 6 percent are Roman Catholic; none are Episcopalian).

First United Methodist Church in Glen Ellyn, Illinois, has adapted Good Sense materials for a class titled Financial Freedom, led by Jason Tews. Tews is the sort of man who has regularly gone missing from churches: driven at work, not normally given to religious reflection, attending worship only occasionally—and then out of family obligation. But he has found a niche at First UMC through the finance class.

Good Sense is devoted primarily to helping people return to financial health, and only secondarily to helping church stewardship campaigns.

Good Sense's most important contribution, he says, is encouraging a change in perspective—helping people see that "it's not our money, it's God's money." Tews has found that many people who attend Financial Freedom class grew up in homes in which money was never discussed. Starting such conversations is no easier now. As one attendee, Richard Dunn, jokingly told me, "We don't talk money much at the church coffee hour."

The lack of small talk about financial worries hardly means that folks don't have such worries. Programs like Financial Freedom fill the need. Tews says he has seen lives changed.

Improved Finances Can Lead to Increased Church Giving

Financial health leads in turn to more faithful support of the church. Barbara Bozgonyi Svoboda told me that the change in mind-set brought about by the course (and the cancellation of credit cards) "really opens up a wide space for giving." Another participant, Jason Pytlik, said he learned that "God's money is on loan to us." Financial Freedom allowed his family to survive a job layoff, pay off some medical expenses, start cutting into old credit debt and start giving to the church.

First UMC's experience with Good Sense materials matches the organization's vision, according to its director at Willow Creek, David Briggs. "We help with finances, but we're more about helping people align their lives differently, to understand the interface between how we relate to money and how we relate to God." Indeed, Good Sense can offer a gracious invitation rather than merely a set of legalistic regulations. Svoboda said budget planning gave her family "permission to get what we wanted and, amazingly, we didn't spend nearly as much as we thought." Dunn expressed amazement at the "innumerable ideas to reduce expenditures" that group members brought to the table.

The Good Sense Web site describes a philosophy of making "the local church teacher a 'hero'"—something that has clearly happened in the case of Tews at First UMC. A crucial part of the program is that a layperson, not the pastor, does this work. When a pastor brings up the topic of money, church members of all stripes are conditioned to assume that it's because the pastor wants more of it from them. Good Sense is devoted primarily to helping people return to financial health, and only secondarily to helping church stewardship campaigns.

"Practically, if individuals or churches pay a lot in debt service, there's less to further the kingdom," Briggs said. "More subtly, we talk about what it means spiritually when you're in bondage to debt."

When I asked Tews whether a secular program couldn't be just as effective in offering this advice, he responded: "What motivation to change would there be without a Christian basis?" But he later granted that other kinds of religious faith could supply a motivation for financial change. "Consumer debt is so out of control," he observed. Financial Freedom classes offer people a chance at recovery—functioning sometimes like an AA [Alcoholics Anonymous] meeting.

Isn't some amount of debt inevitable if one seeks a first-rate education or decides to take a job and live in a high-priced major metropolitan area? On this point, Tews kindly but firmly demurs: "It can be done. It's a question of what's important to you. If you want to give 10 percent, save 10 percent, and live on what's left over, you can. People are almost afraid to be told to do it because they know it's right."

Christian Programs Forge a Support Network

At its best, the Financial Freedom program creates community. It isn't quite like an early Methodist society in which members inquired into the state of one another's soul and whether each had sinned in spending money since the group previously met; Financial Freedom classes don't call for that much disclosure. But the risky act of attending one of the meetings is an admission that one needs help in this area. And sharing wisdom about budgeting and expenditures with fellow members is more profound than everyday church chatter.

On the other hand, it is hard to see why a Christian church, or the worship of its specific crucified and raised Lord, is required for such sharing of financial wisdom. Tews told me his favorite passage to use in class is Proverbs 3:9–10: "Honor the Lord with your substance and with the first fruits of all your produce; then your barns will be filled with plenty, and your vats will be bursting with wine." That is classic wisdom literature, but it could easily encourage a prosperity gospel in which Jesus rewards those who think positive and tithe—a gospel that has little to do with Jesus of Nazareth.

Crown Financial Ministries is the creation of the late evangelical financial adviser Larry Burkett, whose radio broadcast was the cultural forerunner of Ramsey's radio ministry. Burkett's partner, Howard Dayton, long nursed a desire to reach "millions, not thousands" with evangelical financial advice. The group's Web site promises that if Crown meets its goal of reaching 300 million people with its advice, it "will help to fund the Great Commission in a way never seen before." The organization's promotional materials bill it as "the world's largest Christian financial ministry." Its promoters do not think small.

Crown's materials frequently express worry that bankruptcy no longer carries much social stigma. Declaring bankruptcy should only be a last alternative, and the "debtor's motive must he honorable." Ideally, Christians should bear witness to the world by repaying every penny, "even after a bankruptcy." There is nothing here suggesting that predatory lenders share responsibility for consumer debt, in conjunction with politicians who began in the 1970s to curtail government regulations on the lending practices of financial institutions (which is why your penniless cousin keeps getting preapproved-credit card offers). Nor is there any hint that 50 percent of bankruptcies are largely due to medical catastrophes.

To its credit, Crown can turn a critical eye on evangelical culture, as when it points to the hypocrisy of believers who put "subtle pressures on each other to achieve success as a testimony to the Lord's blessings in their lives." But its materials tend to rely on sentences in the conditional mode: "If we place ourselves at His disposal, He will meet our needs and guide us along His paths." Here is the Pelagian danger: it's as though God is sitting around wondering if his creatures will do the right thing so God can dispense (inevitably material) blessings.

Critics Accuse Evangelicals of Using Fear Tactics

A prominent critic of Crown's and Ramsey's approach is investment adviser Gary Moore, who takes issue with the rigid condemnation of consumer debt. He notes that the corporate sponsors of Ramsey's radio show include real estate companies and mortgage lenders. On his Web site, Ramsey acts as pitchman not only for his own financial services but for vitamins and electronics ("You can't afford not to own Tivo!"), encouraging the sort of consumerism he ostensibly seeks to combat.

Moore, who founded the Financial Seminary and served on the board of advisers of the Templeton Foundation, senses a certain fearmongering by Crown and Ramsey in regard to debt. He argues that only 4 percent of consumer credit users are in serious financial trouble and points out the positive side of credit. After the 2004 tsunami, relief money was sent to Indonesia faster than in the case of any other natural disaster in history—because of credit cards. He also points to microcredit initiatives in developing countries as examples of trustworthy, biblical ways in which lending and borrowing can help people out of poverty. "There is a way to lend and borrow biblically—don't charge interest and forgive debts every seven years."

Moore also sees a political agenda behind Crown's and Ramsey's emphasis on debt, noting that they began their jeremiads against the evil of indebtedness during the 1980s and 1990s, when condemnation of "tax and spend" liberals was popular on the political right. (This political sport is not now in favor, since with Republicans at the helm the national debt has risen higher than ever.) And Moore, who sat on the board of the Crystal Cathedral with Enron chief Ken Lay, calls much evangelical financial planning a "combination of Jesus Christ and Ayn Rand": it compartmentalizes money and fundamental theological convictions; so that the manner in which money is raised is unimportant as long as much of it is given to the church.

There is a way to lend and borrow biblically—don't charge interest and forgive debts every seven years.

Finding a Balance Between Spirituality and Consumerism

Evangelical financial ministries can also be charged with thinking too small. They may help middle-class consumers be more practical consumers who, once their books are balanced and they're saving and tithing, can spend freely and without guilt. Consumerism holds out the promise of abundance without limit; its adherents, eternally dissatisfied with what they have, buy more to reassure themselves of their existence. But what if the church, with its claim that Jesus' resurrection inaugurates the end of history and with its view of people's worth as a function of their creation in the image of God, is actually an alternative to capitalism? What if the church should be forming people for more dramatic resistance to consumerism?

Daniel Bell, a theologian at Lutheran Southern Theological Seminary, argues that the gospel is about more than helping people live successfully within consumer capitalism: "I have a simple test I often put before my students. Would Jesus have been crucified for what you are teaching?" He calls on churches to take up the arduous task of shaping people who are not primarily consumers in the first place.

However, Lendol Calder, a historian of consumer debt at Augustana College in Illinois, asserts that the work of evangelical financial advisers, whatever its drawbacks, is important. "The problem of indebtedness is so serious for those caught up in it, and the level of financial literacy in the population so low, that my default attitude toward debt counseling services is one of appreciation for what they're trying to do."

Elizabeth Warren of Harvard Law School takes a similar view. Her book *Two-Income Trap* describes the usurious practices of credit card and mortgage companies, and *All Your Worth: The Ultimate Lifetime Money Plan*, written with her daughter Amelia Warren Tyagi, offers much of the same financial advice as Good Sense, Crown and Ramsey though without the religious references or some of the legalistic judgments. Warren is working with the Lutheran financial organization Thrivent to create a credit counseling plan based on *All Your Worth*. Though her writings have not been explicitly religious, she said, "I believe that no one who is pressed by bills and worried about making it to the end of the month can find spiritual peace."

Added Warren: "Most commentators today seem to divide money and spirituality, keeping them in carefully separated boxes. But I don't think they are separate."

Legislation and Awareness Help Expose Deceptive Tactics of Private Student Loan Issuers

Haley Chitty

Haley Chitty is an associate director of communications for the National Association of Student Financial Aid Administrators.

Financial aid administrators are leading the fight against misleading direct-to-consumer (DTC) marketing of private student loans, but it can feel like a losing battle at times. Fortunately, the recent reauthorization of the Higher Education Act and the efforts of New York Attorney General Andrew Cuomo have given financial aid offices new tools to protect students and parents who borrow private loans to finance higher education.

At best, private education loans can provide students and parents with much needed additional funds to enable them to pay for higher education.

At worst, private loans can be exploited by predatory lenders who pressure students and parents into excessive borrowing through high-interest loans that can make them ineligible for other, less expensive, financial aid.

Private Loans Might Make Students Ineligible for Other Aid

Any financial aid administrator can provide the anecdotal evidence of the poor student who is awarded a private loan with a 16 percent interest rate that exceeds the institution's cost of attendance (COA), causing the student to lose out on other financial aid.

Aggregate data on private loans can be hard to come by because these loans encompass the fastest growing sector of college financial aid, and because they are sometimes made without the financial aid office knowing about them. The American Council on Education (ACE) compiled some data on private loans. While the data is not complete, it offers a glimpse into some of the problems with these loans.

At worst, private loans can be exploited by predatory lenders who pressure students and parents into excessive borrowing through high-interest loans.

According to ACE analysis of the U.S. Department of Education's National Postsecondary Student Aid Study (NPSAS) data:

- More than 10 percent of private loan borrowers don't apply for other types of aid.

- Nearly 25 percent of private loan borrowers did not borrow a Federal Stafford Loan.

- Excluding students who don't meet federal student loan eligibility requirements (such as noncitizens), 20 percent of undergraduate private loan borrowers did not take advantage of federal student loans before borrowing private loans. Half of these students did not file the required application for federal student loans.

Many of the students and parents who fall victim to DTC marketing of private student loans do not receive counseling from the financial aid office. Because private loans are sometimes made directly to students, the financial aid office may not ever know the student is receiving these funds.

Legislation Provides Increased Protection

Although Congress did not implement all the borrower protections advocated by the National Association of Student Financial Aid Administrators and most of the higher education community, the Higher Education Opportunity Act (HEOA) did make some inroads to protect borrowers from the negative consequences of borrowing private student loans.

Because private loans are sometimes made directly to students, the financial aid office may not ever know the student is receiving these funds.

Signed into law in August [2008], the HEOA restricts some private loan marketing that can be misleading and requires lenders to disclose significantly more information about private loan alternatives. Congress considered provisions that would have required private loans to be certified by the financial aid office and allowed private loans to be discharged in bankruptcy. Although these provisions would have provided greater protection for students and parents, they did not make it into the final version of the bill.

Instead, the new law requires that borrowers self-certify their private loans. The secretary of education is directed to work with the Board of Governors of the Federal Reserve System to develop a self-certification form for private loans. This form will disclose to students that:

- Private loan applicants may qualify for federal, state, or institutional aid instead of (or in addition to) private loans.

- Students should consult with the financial aid office about other forms of financial aid available.

- Private loans may affect eligibility for free or lower costing financial aid.

The form will also require the private loan applicant to provide:

- The applicant's cost of attendance (COA) and expected family contribution (EFC).

- Estimated financial assistance from family.

- The difference between the COA and estimated financial assistance.

Students will also learn from the form that the required information is available from the financial aid office.

The HEOA allows borrowers to cancel a private loan without any penalty within three business days of the loan's being completed. The law also provides borrowers with a 30-day period to accept the terms of a private loan and requires that the terms of that loan cannot change during that period.

While Congress did not provide all the protections for which the higher education community advocated, the protections passed will help private loan borrowers make more informed decisions and provide additional opportunities for financial aid offices to counsel students and families before they borrow.

Implementing a Code of Conduct for Private Loan Companies

In another victory for financial aid offices fighting misleading information disseminated by some private loan providers, on September 11 [2008] eight DTC student loan providers agreed to a code of conduct developed by New York Attorney General Andrew Cuomo.

Cuomo began investigating DTC private loan providers in October 2007 by issuing subpoenas to EduCap, Affinity Direct/ Educational Direct, and three DTC brands of the First Marblehead Corporation. Cuomo said he was pursuing DTC marketers because of consumer advocates who complained about loan companies that were bombarding borrowers with misleading direct mailings, telemarketing calls, and web and television advertising.

"This industry has a spotty track record when it comes to protecting consumers, and it's time for the companies to be held responsible," said Cuomo in a press statement.

Some of the deceptive practices uncovered by the Cuomo investigation included:

- Logos that appeared to be from the federal government.

- False checks and rebates to entice students to borrow loans from these providers.

- Illegal inducements and prizes meant to distract students from the terms and conditions of the loans.

- Inducements that encouraged students to recruit their friends to take out similar loans.

- Advertising that misrepresented the terms and conditions of the loans and a failure to guarantee the advertised borrower benefits.

Under the settlement, lenders are prohibited from using any of those tactics and must provide students with a disclaimer that they should exhaust all of their federal student loan options before turning to private student loans.

Institutions can encourage the lenders they work with to adopt this new code of conduct to reduce the number of students making bad private student loan choices.

Colleges Need to Raise Awareness About Deceptive Practices

Administrators at higher ed[ucation] institutions can better protect their students from the negative consequences of DTC private loan marketing by collaborating to raise awareness of these loans. For starters, the financial aid office should not be alone in efforts to help students avoid private loan pitfalls.

Administrators in other campus offices should be knowledgeable about the issues related to DTC loan marketing so they can refer students to the financial aid office if they are suspicious that a student is taking out a private loan without knowing all the facts.

For example, a student may ask the registrar for proof of enrollment in order to get a private loan. The registrar should ask the student about the purpose of the proof of enrollment, and direct him or her to the financial aid office if it is for a private loan.

Campuswide collaboration, combined with new protections in the HEOA and a new marketing code of conduct, will help ensure that students make better borrowing decisions and avoid the pitfalls of uninformed borrowing.

Debt Collection Agencies Should Not Be Allowed to Harass Debtors

Charles Phelan

Charles Phelan is a consumer debt consultant. He is the author of Debt Elimination Success Seminar, *an audio-CD program that teaches consumers how to choose debt programs based on their financial situations.*

If you are behind on your bills and on the receiving end of collection phone calls, you will probably hear collectors make some very threatening statements. While most debt collection professionals try to stay within the boundaries defined by the Federal Fair Debt Collection Practices Act (FDCPA), many others cross the line on a regular basis. Last year [2005], the Federal Trade Commission [FTC] received more than 58,000 complaints about debt collectors, a figure that represents 17% of the total number of complaints received by the FTC. Consumers complain about the collection industry more than most other industries combined.

Collection professionals would probably respond that the enormous size of the industry and the sheer volume of collection activity accounts for the large number of complaints. However, only a small percentage of violations are actually reported by consumers, so the data collected by the FTC represent only a tiny fraction of the true scope of the problem. Even so, a pattern of abusive and illegal collection activity has been well-documented by the FTC, and it is getting worse instead of better.

Charles Phelan, "When Debt Collectors Cross the Line," Buzzle.com, January 14, 2006. Reproduced by permission.

Collectors Use Scare Tactics to Threaten Debtors

Here are some common threats made by debt collectors:

"We're going to take your house unless you pay this bill immediately." This is a bogus threat. Unless the debt being collected is secured by the house in question (i.e., a mortgage or home equity loan), the creditor does not have the power to take your house away from you.

"If you don't pay this bill today, we're going to have a warrant issued for your arrest." Nonsense. Failure to pay a debt is a civil matter, not a criminal matter. Threatening a debtor with jail time or accusing them of committing a crime is totally against the rules.

"We don't care that you sent a cease communication notice. We're going to call you anyway." The FDCPA gives you the right to terminate contact efforts by a debt collector. Failure to respect a cease communication notice is a clear violation of Federal law.

Threatening a debtor with jail time or accusing them of committing a crime is totally against the rules.

"We're going to garnish your wages to recover this debt." A collector can only threaten action it has the legal authority to take, and the vast majority of collection agencies have zero legal authority. Your wages can only be garnished by a creditor after they have won a judgment against you in a lawsuit.

"We know where you live, so you better pay up." Yes, threats of violence still happen in this industry. Nearly 300 complaints against collectors received by the FTC last year cited the threat of violence as the cause of the complaint. This is absolutely illegal.

Some Collectors Harass Family, Friends, and Employers

Aside from the usual bogus threats, collectors also use other tactics that are illegal. For example, discussing your debt with a third party is a clear violation of the FDCPA. Yet collectors routinely call neighbors, relatives, and employers to obtain information on debtors. So long as the collector does not discuss the actual matter of the debt, they still have their toes on the right side of the line. But as soon as they mention or even hint that they are calling about a debt, they have crossed the line.

Since many debtors have taken to screening their phone calls at home to cut down on the relentless barrage, debt collectors frequently call at work when they can obtain an office number. In theory, a consumer can get the collector to stop calling at the office simply by stating that they are not allowed to receive personal phone calls at work. That puts the collector on notice that such activity constitutes interference with the consumer's employment, which is not permitted. In practice, however, collectors routinely ignore this rule and continue to call at work.

There are many other techniques of harassment and intimidation that cross the line from permissible to impermissible collection activity. Use of obscene or profane language, shouting, constant and unrelenting telephone calls, failure to respond to written disputes, and publication of debtor information all constitute illegal activity as defined by the FDCPA.

Debtors Have the Right to Protect Themselves

So if you are on the receiving end of illegal collection actions, what can you do to protect yourself? First and foremost, it's important to know and understand your rights as a consumer. A description of your rights under The Fair Debt Collection

Practices Act may be obtained directly from the FTC: http://www.ftc.gov/bcp/conline/pubs/credit/fdc.htm.

If you believe that a collector has violated your rights in their attempt to collect from you, then you should not hesitate to file formal complaints with the Attorney General for your state (www.naag.org) as well as the Federal Trade Commission. If enough complaints are received about a particular collector, these authorities are empowered to bring an enforcement action against them, which may result in expensive fines that will make the agency or collector think twice about using such tactics in the future. You also have the right to bring a lawsuit yourself against a collector that harasses or abuses you, or otherwise violates your rights under the law.

One final point. The FDCPA technically only applies to third-party debt collectors, which includes collection agencies and collection attorneys. It does not apply to the original creditor when collecting their own debt. For example, if you borrow money from a bank, the bank is not regulated by the FDCPA. However, numerous other public laws protect consumers from deceptive or abusive collection practices even by original creditors, and many states also have laws that parallel the FDCPA but go further and include original creditors in the definition of debt collector. So if an original creditor is harassing you or has crossed the line, you should still file a complaint with your state's Attorney General as well as [with] the FTC. If a clear pattern of abuse emerges, the original creditor can be charged with unfair or deceptive acts or practices, either under state law or under the FTC Act that governs conduct of commerce in our country.

To sum up, if you are on the receiving end of collection harassment, don't just take it. Educate yourself on your rights as a consumer, vigorously dispute debts that you don't believe you owe, and take action yourself in the form of complaints to your Attorney General and the Federal Trade Commission. By standing up for your rights, you can put a stop to bogus threats and illegal collection tactics.

The Government Should Create a Commission to Monitor the Financial Services Industry

Elizabeth Warren

Elizabeth Warren is the Leo Gottlieb Professor of Law at Harvard Law School. She also is the chair of the Congressional Oversight Panel created to monitor the government bailout of the U.S. banking industry, the program known as the Troubled Assets Relief Program (TARP). She is the co-author of The Two-Income Trap: Why Middle-Class Mothers and Fathers Are Going Broke *and* All Your Worth: The Ultimate Lifetime Money Plan.

It is impossible to buy a toaster that has a one-in-five chance of bursting into flames and burning down your house. But it is possible to refinance an existing home with a mortgage that has the same one-in-five chance of putting the family out on the street—and the mortgage won't even carry a disclosure of that fact to the homeowner. Similarly, it's impossible to change the price on a toaster once it has been purchased. But long after the papers have been signed, it is possible to triple the price of the credit used to finance the purchase of that appliance, even if the customer meets all the credit terms, in full and on time. Why are consumers safe when they purchase tangible consumer products with cash, but when they sign up for routine financial products like mortgages and credit cards they are left at the mercy of their creditors?

The difference between the two markets is regulation. Although considered an epithet in Washington since Ronald Reagan swept into the White House, the "R-word" supports a

Elizabeth Warren, "Unsafe at Any Rate," *Democracy Journal*, Summer 2007, pp. 8–9, 14–19. Reproduced by permission.

booming market in tangible consumer goods. Nearly every product sold in America has passed basic safety regulations well in advance of reaching store shelves. Credit products, by comparison, are regulated by a tattered patchwork of federal and state laws that have failed to adapt to changing markets. Moreover, thanks to effective regulation, innovation in the market for physical products has led to more safety and cutting-edge features. By comparison, innovation in financial products has produced incomprehensible terms and sharp practices that have left families at the mercy of those who write the contracts.

Consumers Need Protection from Unethical Lenders

Sometimes consumer trust in a creditor is well-placed. Indeed, credit has provided real value for millions of households, permitting the purchase of homes that can add to family wealth accumulation and cars that can expand job opportunities. Credit can also provide a critical safety net and a chance for a family to borrow against a better tomorrow when they hit job layoffs, medical problems, or family break-ups today. Other financial products, such as life insurance and annuities, also can greatly enhance a family's security. Consumers might not spend hours pouring over the details of their credit card terms or understand every paper they signed at a real estate closing, but many of those financial products are offered on fair terms that benefit both seller and customer.

But for a growing number of families who are steered into over-priced credit products, risky subprime mortgages, and misleading insurance plans, trust in a creditor turns out to be costly. And for families who get tangled up with truly dangerous financial products, the result can be wiped-out savings, lost homes, higher costs for car insurance, denial of jobs, troubled marriages, bleak retirements, and broken lives.

Consumers can enter the market to buy physical products confident that they won't be tricked into buying exploding toasters and other unreasonably dangerous products. They can concentrate their shopping efforts in other directions, helping to drive a competitive market that keeps costs low and encourages innovation in convenience, durability, and style. Consumers entering the market to buy financial products should enjoy the same protection. Just as the Consumer Product Safety Commission (CPSC) protects buyers of goods and supports a competitive market, we need the same for consumers of financial products—a new regulatory regime, and even a new regulatory body, to protect consumers who use credit cards, home mortgages, car loans, and a host of other products. The time has come to put scaremongering to rest and to recognize that regulation can often support and advance efficient and more dynamic markets.

The time has come to put scaremongering to rest and to recognize that regulation can often support and advance efficient and more dynamic markets.

Traditional Regulation Does Not Go Far Enough

The credit industry is not without regulation; credit transactions have been regulated by statute or common law since the founding of the Republic. Traditionally, states bore the primary responsibility for protecting their citizens from unscrupulous lenders, imposing usury caps and other credit regulations on all companies doing business locally. While states still play some role, particularly in the regulation of real-estate transactions, their primary tool—interest rate regulation—has been effectively destroyed by federal legislation. Today, any lender that gets a federal bank charter can locate its operations in a state with high usury rates (e.g., South Dakota or

Delaware), then export that states' interest rate caps (or no caps at all) to customers located all over the country. As a result, and with no public debate, interest rates have been effectively deregulated across the country, leaving the states powerless to act. In April of this year [2007], the Supreme Court took another step in the same direction in *Watters v. Wachovia*, giving federal regulators the power to shut down state efforts to regulate mortgage lenders without providing effective federal regulation to replace it.

Local laws suffer from another problem. As lenders have consolidated and credit markets have gone national, a plethora of state regulations drives up costs for lenders, forcing them to include repetitive disclosures and meaningless exceptions in order to comply with differing local laws, even as it also leaves open regulatory gaps. The resulting patchwork of regulation is neither effective nor cost-effective. During the 1970s and early 1980s, for instance, Congress moved the regulation of some aspects of consumer credit from the state to the federal level through a series of landmark bills that included Truth-in-Lending (TIL), Fair Credit Reporting, and anti-discrimination regulations. These statutes tend to be highly specific. TIL, for example, specifies the information that must be revealed in a credit transaction, including the size of the typeface that must be used and how interest rates must be stated. But the specificity of these laws works against their effectiveness, trapping the regulations like a fly in amber. The statutes inhibit some beneficial innovations (e.g., new ways of informing consumers) while they fail to regulate dangerous innovations (e.g., no discussion of negative amortization). What's more, these generation-old regulations completely miss most of the new features of credit products, such as universal default, double-cycle billing, and other changes in credit.

Any effort to increase or reform statutory regulation of financial products is met by a powerful industry lobby on one side that is not balanced by an equally effective consumer lobby on the other. As a result, even the most basic efforts are blocked from becoming law. A decade ago, for example, mortgage-lender abuses were rare. Today, experts estimate that fraud and deception have stripped $9.1 billion in equity from homeowners, particularly from elderly and working-class families. A few hearty souls have repeatedly introduced legislation to halt such practices, but those bills never make it out of committee.

Beyond Congress, some regulation of financial products occurs through the indirect mechanism of the Federal Reserve, the Office of the Comptroller of the Currency (OCC), and the Office of Thrift Supervision. Each agency, for example, has some power to control certain forms of predatory lending. But their main mission is to protect the financial stability of banks and other financial institutions, not to protect consumers. As a result, they focus intently on bank profitability and far less on the financial impact on customers of many of the products the banks sell.

Any effort to increase or reform statutory regulation of financial products is met by a powerful industry lobby on one side that is not balanced by an equally effective consumer lobby on the other.

Lenders Know How to Subvert the System

The current regulatory jumble creates another problem: Consumer financial products are regulated based, principally, on the identity of the issuer, rather than the nature of the product. The subprime mortgage market provides a stunning example of the resulting fractured oversight. In 2005, for example, 23 percent of subprime mortgages were issued by regulated thrifts and banks. Another 25 percent were issued by bank holding companies, which were subject to different regulatory oversight through the federal system. But more than half—52 percent, to be exact—of all subprime mortgages originated with companies with no federal supervision at all, largely stand-alone mortgage brokers and finance companies. This division not only creates enormous loopholes, it also triggers a kind of regulatory arbitrage. Regulators are acutely aware that if they push financial institutions too hard, those institutions will simply reincorporate in another form under the umbrella of a different regulatory agency—or no regulatory agency at all. Indeed, in recent years a number of credit unions have dissolved and reincorporated as state or national banks, precisely to fit under a regulatory charter that would give them different options in developing and marketing financial products. If the regulated have the option to choose their regulators, then it should be no surprise when they game the rules in their own favor.

Financial products should be subject to the same routine safety screening that now governs the sale of every toaster, washing machine, and child's car seat sold on the American market.

Unfortunately, in a world in which the financial services industry is routinely one of the top three contributors to national political campaigns, giving $133 million over the past five years, the likelihood of quick action to respond to specific problems and to engage in meaningful oversight is vanishingly slim. The resulting splintered regulatory framework has created regulatory loopholes and timid regulators. This leaves the American consumer effectively unprotected in a world in which a number of merchants of financial products have shown themselves very willing to take as much as they can by any means they can.

How the Financial Product Safety Commission Would Work

Clearly, it is time for a new model of financial regulation, one focused primarily on consumer safety rather than corporate profitability. Financial products should be subject to the same routine safety screening that now governs the sale of every toaster, washing machine, and child's car seat sold on the American market.

The model for such safety regulation is the U.S. Consumer Product Safety Commission (CPSC), an independent health and safety regulatory agency founded in 1972 by the [Richard] Nixon Administration. The CPSC's mission is to protect the American public from risks of injury and death from products used in the home, school, and recreation. The agency has the authority to develop uniform safety standards, order the recall of unsafe products, and ban products that pose unreasonable risks. In establishing the Commission, Congress recognized that "the complexities of consumer products and the diverse nature and abilities of consumers using them frequently result in an inability of users to anticipate risks and to safeguard themselves adequately."

The evidence clearly shows that CPSC is a cost-effective agency. Since it was established, product-related death and injury rates in the United States have decreased substantially. The CPSC estimates that just three safety standards for three products alone—cigarette lighters, cribs, and baby walkers—save more than $2 billion annually. The annual estimated savings is more than CPSC's total cumulative budget since its inception.

So why not create a Financial Product Safety Commission (FPSC)? Like its counterpart for ordinary consumer products, this agency would be charged with responsibility to establish guidelines for consumer disclosure, collect and report data about the uses of different financial products, review new financial products for safety, and require modification of dangerous products before they can be marketed to the public. The agency could review mortgages, credit cards, car loans, and a number of other financial products, such as life insurance and annuity contracts. In effect, the FPSC would evaluate these products to eliminate the hidden tricks and traps that make some of them far more dangerous than others.

An Industry Watchdog Would Benefit Consumers

An FPSC would promote the benefits of free markets by assuring that consumers can enter credit markets with confidence that the products they purchase meet minimum safety standards. No one expects every customer to become an engineer to buy a toaster that doesn't burst into flames, or analyze complex diagrams to buy an infant car seat that doesn't collapse on impact. By the same reasoning, no customer should be forced to read the fine print in 30-plus-page credit card contracts to determine whether the company claims it can seize property paid for with the credit card or raise the interest rate by more than 20 points if the customer gets into a dispute with the water company.

Instead, an FPSC would develop precisely such expertise in consumer financial products. A commission would be able to collect data about which financial products are least understood, what kinds of disclosures are most effective, and which products are most likely to result in consumer default. Free of legislative micromanaging, it could develop nuanced regulatory responses; some terms might be banned altogether, while others might be permitted only with clearer disclosure. A Commission might promote uniform disclosures that make it easier to compare products from one issuer to another, and to discern conflicts of interest on the part of a mortgage broker or seller of a currently loosely regulated financial product. In the area of credit card regulation, for example, an FPSC might want to review the following terms that appear in some—but not all—credit card agreements: universal clauses; unlimited and unexplained fees; interest rate increases that exceed 10 percentage points; and an issuer's claim that it can change the terms of cards after money has been borrowed. It would also promote such market-enhancing practices as a simple, easy-to-read paragraph that explains all interest charges; clear explanations of when fees will be imposed; a requirement that the terms of a credit card remain the same until the card expires; no marketing targeted at college students or people under age 21; and a statement showing how long it will take to pay off the balance, as well as how much interest will be paid if the customer makes the minimum monthly payments on the outstanding balance on a credit card.

With every agency, the fear of regulatory capture is ever-present. But in a world in which there is little coherent, consumer-oriented regulation of any kind, an FPSC with power to act is far better than the available alternatives. Whether it is housed in a current agency like the CPSC or stands alone, the point is to concentrate the review of financial products in a single location, with a focus on the safety of the products as consumers use them. Companies that offer good products would have little to fear. Indeed, if they could conduct business without competing with companies whose business model involves misleading the customer, then the companies offering safer products would be more likely to flourish. Moreover, with an FPSC, consumer credit companies would be free to innovate on a level playing field within the boundaries of clearly disclosed terms and open competition—not hidden terms designed to mislead consumers.

The consumer financial services industry has grown to more than $3 trillion in annual business. Lenders employ thousands of lawyers, marketing agencies, statisticians, and business strategists to help them increase profits. In a rapidly changing market, customers need someone on their side to help make certain that the financial products they buy meet minimum safety standards. A Financial Product Safety Commission would be the consumers' ally.

When a lender can bury a sentence at the bottom of 47 lines of text saying it can change any term at any time for any reason, the market is broken.

The Goal Is to Create a Well-Regulated Market

When markets work, they produce value for both buyers and sellers, both borrowers and lenders. But the basic premise of any free market is full information. When a lender can bury a sentence at the bottom of 47 lines of text saying it can change any term at any time for any reason, the market is broken.

Product safety standards will not fix every problem associated with consumer credit. It is possible to stuff a toaster with dirty socks and start a fire, and, even with safety standards, it will remain possible to get burned by credit products. Some people won't even have to try very hard. But safety standards can make a critical difference for millions of families. Families who are steered into higher-priced mortgages solely because the broker wanted a higher fee would have a greater chance of buying—and keeping—a home. A student who wanted a credit card with a firm credit limit—not an approval for thousands of dollars more of credit and higher fees and interest—could stay out of trouble. An older person who needed a little cash to make it until her Social Security check arrived would have a manageable loan, not one that would escalate into thousands of dollars in fees.

Industry practices would change as well. Corporate profit models based on marketing mortgages with a one-in-five chance of costing a family its home would stop. Credit card models that lure 18-year-olds with no income and no credit history into debt with promises of "no parental approval"—on the assumption that their parents will pay it off, rather than see their children begin their adult lives with ruined credit histories—would stop. Rollovers that can turn a simple loan into a mountain of debt would stop.

Personal responsibility will always play a critical role in dealing with credit cards, just as personal responsibility remains a central feature in the safe use of any other product. But a Financial Product Safety Commission could eliminate some of the most egregious tricks and traps in the credit industry. And for every family who avoids a trap or doesn't get caught by a trick, that's regulation that works.

Payday Lenders Should Not Be Allowed to Charge Exorbitant Interest Rates

Jonathan P. Baird

Jonathan P. Baird is an attorney and lobbyist for New Hampshire Legal Assistance.

While it would be easy to think payday lending is some new phenomenon, nothing could be further from the truth. Payday lending is the modern form of usury. Usury and its regulation have been the subject of civil and religious debate for literally thousands of years.

Usury is not a word you hear used very often now. It has a musty, 19th-century quality. Usury can mean the price paid for the use of money. It can also simply mean excessive interest.

State usury laws refer to a body of law regulating the amount of interest charged by lenders. Most states have long had laws specifying the maximum legal interest rates at which loans can be made. For almost our entire history as a state, until 1999, New Hampshire has had such laws protecting consumers.

In January [2008], the Legislature will take up House Bill 267, a bill placing an interest rate cap of 36 percent APR [annual percentage rate] on payday and auto title loans. The bill is modeled on legislation passed by Congress in 2006 to protect our military service members who were being victimized by payday lenders. It would restore an interest rate cap that has been our state norm.

There is a long history dating back to before the American Revolution of the use of interest rate caps to protect against usury. In his excellent book, *Taming the Sharks*, law professor Christopher Peterson recounts this history.

A Long History of Regulating Usury

Originally, the colonies imported English law, which included an interest rate cap statute called the Statute of Anne. It imposed a maximum allowable interest rate of 5 percent per year. Most of the states initially imposed caps between 4 and 10 percent per year, although after independence most states set their maximum rate at 6 percent per year.

Early American society featured a very strong thrift ethic. Reckless borrowing for personal consumption was extremely frowned upon. The public had little sympathy for debtors. State law rigorously enforced debts and a sense of shame attached to personal debt. This was the era of debtors' prisons. Even though low interest rates were the norm, imprisonment for debt was very common. In Massachusetts in 1830, there were three to five times as many persons imprisoned for debt as for crime.

After the Civil War, attitudes toward personal debt loosened. A new lending practice developed called salary lending—the historic precursor of payday lending. The principle was the same. A debtor would borrow $5 and repay $6 at the end of the week.

While that might not sound too bad to modern ears, it led to chain debt, an early version of the repeat borrowing trap characteristic of payday loans. Manipulative lender practices like the imposition of staggering late fees and shady calculation of interest trapped debtors into endless payments.

Salary lending was characterized by lenders collecting the most money while reducing the overall debt owed as little as possible. If the debtor lost his job or suffered illness or could not pay for some other reason, interest compounded and debt swelled.

The salary lenders targeted employed and married working class white men, seeing them as good credit risks and likely to repay because of their steady employment histories.

Salary Lenders Were the First Loan Sharks

The term "loan-sharking" did not originate with the 20th-century Mafia. It actually comes from the period after the Civil War. In the Eastern cities, the salary lenders were infamous for charging interest rates over 1,000 percent annually.

The abuses and horror stories about this loan-sharking led to a series of governmental reforms and policy responses. Federal bankruptcy law reform allowing more discharge of debt, an increase in cooperative and charitable lending, and new small loan laws were all responses to the havoc created by usury.

The 20th century saw an explosion of credit and greatly expanded consumer debt. Old American stigmas about reckless borrowing disappeared and the credit card made its appearance.

In contrast to the New Deal period, when government took a wide range of regulatory, protective steps, government since the [Ronald] Reagan era has promoted deregulation, which opened the door to exploitation of the poor.

It is a sign of our moral confusion that we do not readily see payday lending as a gross form of usury.

No Limit on Interest Rates

When interest rate caps were scrapped in our state in 1999, the legislative history shows that the Legislature expected interest rates to go up to only 20 to 25 percent. There was no expectation interest rates would soar into the stratospheric rates of the payday lenders where the sky is the limit.

Five hundred percent APR? No problem if you are a payday lender. It is a sign of our moral confusion that we do not readily see payday lending as a gross form of usury. There are reasons the Christian, Jewish, and Islamic traditions have all rejected usury as pure, unchecked greed. I expect ethical atheists would too.

This is not some moderately priced consumer credit. While payday lenders and auto title lenders strive for acceptance and legitimacy, they are 21st-century loan sharks. This is the dark side of deregulation where the administrative state has failed and consumer protection has been junked.

The issues around payday lending are just the latest round in an American fight over predatory lending that has been longstanding. No strategy will completely stop the payday lenders. They are foxy and will try to work around legislation. Still, restoring an interest rate cap is the time-tested reform which has proven most effective in curbing abusive money lending.

CHAPTER 4

Is Declaring Bankruptcy a Good Way to Handle Too Much Debt?

Overview: The Dramatic Rise in Personal Bankruptcies

Thomas A. Garrett

Thomas A. Garrett is a research officer at the Federal Reserve Bank of St. Louis.

Personal bankruptcy filings in the United States increased, per capita, nearly 350 percent between 1980 and 2005. This paper first addresses the changes in economic and institutional factors that have occurred over the past 100 years, many of which have occurred in the past 30 years, which are likely contributors to the dramatic rise in personal bankruptcy filings seen across the country. These factors include a reduction in personal savings, an increase in consumer debt, the proliferation of revolving credit, changes to bankruptcy law, and a reduced social stigma associated with filing for bankuptcy. Given the availability of bankruptcy data at various levels of aggregation, the remaining sections of the paper contain results from several different empirical analyses of bankruptcy filings using various data sets. Careful attention is paid to personal bankruptcy filings in counties located in Eighth Federal Reserve District states. (JEL D14, K35, G33)

Personal bankruptcy filings in the United States have soared over the past 30 years, from 1.2 per 1,000 persons in 1980 to nearly 5.4 per 1,000 persons in 2005, an increase of nearly 350 percent. Over this period, bankruptcies have been growing at an average annual rate of nearly 7 percent, about 1.5 times greater than the average rate of annual per capita gross domestic product (GDP) growth. Taking a longer perspective

Thomas A. Garrett, "The Rise in Personal Bankruptcies: The Eighth Federal Reserve District and Beyond," *Federal Reserve Bank of St. Louis Review*, vol. 89, no. 1, January/February 2007, pp. 15–17, 19–22, 36–37. Copyright © 2007 Federal Reserve Bank of St. Louis. Reproduced by permission.

the 2005 filing rate of 5.4 per 1,000 persons is nearly 80 times greater than the 1920 rate of 0.06 filings per 1,000 persons.[1]

These statistics disguise the fact that personal bankruptcy filings are not equal across the country. For example, at the state level, Tennessee has usually had the highest rate of personal bankruptcy filings in the nation, with over 10 filings per 1,000 persons.[2] Shelby County in Tennessee (Memphis area) led the nation in personal bankruptcy filings, with a rate of over 20 filings per 1,000 persons, or 2 percent of the population of Shelby County. At the other end of the spectrum, Massachusetts had a filing rate of 2.8 filings per 1,000 persons, ranking last of all states.

So what is behind this rapid increase in bankruptcy filings? The general cause of most personal bankruptcy filings is no mystery: An individual has too much debt and often also experiences an unexpected negative shock to his or her income, such as divorce, unemployment, or an uncovered medical expense. But this does not explain the increase in personal bankruptcy filings that has occurred over the past 100 years, nor does it explain the explosive growth in bankruptcy filings over the past 30 years.

The first part of this paper will discuss changes in several economic and institutional factors that are likely contributors to the dramatic rise in personal bankruptcy filings seen across the country. An examination of these factors may help clarify the causes of increased bankruptcy filings and may thus lead to a better understanding of the solutions to reverse this trend.

The availability of bankruptcy data at various levels of aggregatlon—that is, national, state, and local—affords us the opportunity to conduct temporal and cross-sectional analyses

1. Bankruptcy data are from the Administrative Office of the U.S. Courts: www.uscourts.gov/adminoff.html.
2. Tennessee ranked third in personal bankruptcies in 2005—bankruptcies per 1,000 persons were greater in Indiana and Ohio in 2005.

of bankruptcy filings at these different levels of aggregation. The remaining section of the paper will present and discuss the results from several different empirical analyses of bankruptcy filings using various data sets. Analysis at the national level will explore the long-run versus short-run relationship between bankruptcy filings and several key economic variables, such as the savings rate, consumer debt, and income. An analysis of state-level personal bankruptcy filings reveals that bankruptcy filing rates have been converging over time. That is, states having had higher personal bankruptcy filings are found to have had lower rates of growth in bankruptcy filings. Finally, analysis at the county level uses data for all counties in Eighth Federal Reserve District states. The county analysis explores the relationship of personal bankruptcy filings with income and the distribution of income.

A Brief History of Bankruptcy Law in the United States

The U.S. Constitution gives Congress the authority to legislate bankruptcy. Article I, Section 8 of the Constitution reads "The Congress shall have Power To establish . . . uniform Laws on the subject of Bankruptcies throughout the United States." Despite this Constitutional authority, no permanent bankruptcy law existed in the United States for the first 120 years after this country's founding.[3]

Three federal bankruptcy acts were passed—in 1800, 1841, and 1867—but all were repealed shortly after their enactment for several reasons. First, during the late 1700s and most of the 1800s, the demand for bankruptcy legislation by debtors and creditors increased during recessionary periods and diminished during boom periods. Second, strong political divides in Congress between Whigs and Federalists (Republicans), who were pro-creditor, and Democrats, who

---

3. A detailed history of bankruptcy legislation in the United States can be found in Skeel (2001) and www.princeton.edu/~pefinmar/Hansen.pdf.

were pro-debtor, prevented the permanency of any legislation. Third, the process of filing for bankruptcy under each of the three acts was far from easy—a costly administrative structure was in place and all bankruptcy filings had to be done in one of the relatively small number of federal courts across the country.

The first long-lasting piece of bankruptcy legislation in the United States was the 1898 Bankruptcy Act. The 1898 Act was designed to aid creditors in the liquidation of an individual's assets and reorganize insolvent corporations. At the time of the 1898 Act, corporate bankruptcies accounted for the vast majority of all bankruptcy filings. Unlike the earlier acts of 1800, 1841, and 1867, the permanency of the 1898 Act was due to (i) a unified Congress and presidency (Republican) and (ii) the rapid growth and political strength of special interest groups (pro-debtor and pro-creditor) that culminated in the late 1800s. The rise of populism through the 1800s contributed to a strong political demand for pro-debtor bankruptcy legislation. On the other hand, the growth in business and industry over this same time period resulted in the rise of pro-business interest groups such as chambers of commerce and commercial trade groups. Competition between these growing interest groups placed great political pressures on Congress to pass long-lasting bankruptcy legislation. The 1898 Act also fostered the growth of professional bankruptcy groups that had tremendous political influence, such as the American Bar Association and Community Law League.

No permanent bankruptcy law existed in the United States for the first 120 years after this country's founding.

The Great Depression in the 1930s revealed several problems with the 1898 Bankruptcy Act.[4] First, the percentage of voluntary personal bankruptcy filings grew at this time. The

1898 Act, while containing some provisions for personal bank-ruptcy filing, mostly addressed the issue of corporate bank-ruptcy. Second, the 1898 Act stipulated that all corporations that filed for bankruptcy be placed in corporate receivership.[5] Increased business bankruptcies during the Great Depression revealed several problems, including corruption, with the structure of corporate receivership established under the 1898 Act.

The Chandler Act of 1938 was designed to remedy weak-nesses of the 1898 Bankruptcy Act. Many more provisions for individual and corporate debtors were contained in the Chan-dler Act. For example, it allowed debtors to choose between liquidation and repayment of debt and also provided for vol-untary and involuntary bankruptcy filings. As with the 1898 Act, the impetus behind the Chandler Act was the strong de-sire of various special interest groups, such as the American Bar Association, National Association of Credit Management, and the Commercial Law League, to change federal bank-ruptcy law.

The next significant piece of bankruptcy legislation was the Bankruptcy Reform Act of 1978. Between the 1930s and 1970s, corporate bankruptcy filings decreased but personal bankruptcies steadily increased. The 1978 Act (also known as the "Bankruptcy Code") replaced many earlier provisions for voluntary personal bankruptcy established by the 1898 Act. Individuals could choose between Chapter 7 filing, which pro-vided for the liquidation of the debtor's assets, or Chapter 13, which allowed for the repayment and reorganization of a debtor's assets.[6] Many of the changes to Chapter 13 made bankruptcy a more attractive option to debtors than in the

---

4. See http://oh.net/encyclopedia/article/hansen.bankruptcy.law.us.
5. A receiver is a person or company appointed to manage a corporation during its re-organization.
6. See Nelson (1999) on consumers' choice between filing Chapter 7 or Chapter 13.

past, and it is argued by some that the 1978 Act caused, at least in part, the increase in bankruptcy filings immediately following implementation of the Act.[7]

Additional changes to the 1978 Act were made by the Bankruptcy Reform Act of 1994, such as expediting the procedures for personal and corporate bankruptcy filings and increasing the percentage of a debtor's assets that are exempt from creditors (called the homestead exemption).

President George W. Bush signed the Bankruptcy Abuse Prevention and Consumer Protection Act of 2005 into law on April 20, 2005, with the Act taking effect on October 17, 2005. The Act was designed to reduce the number of personal bankruptcy filings that have continued to increase since the late 1970s, by increasing the cost of filings for personal bankruptcy.[8] Specifically, the 2005 Act introduces two needs-based tests (based on income) for Chapter 7 filings (liquidations), requires filers to participate in credit counseling, and increases the allowable time between Chapter 7 filings to 8 years. The Act also established several requirements for lenders, such as better disclosure regarding minimum payments, interest rates (on credit cards), late payment deadlines, and introductory rates. The 2005 Act was seen by consumers as increasing the costs of filing for bankruptcy; consequently, filing rates increased dramatically (nearly six times higher than average) prior to the Act's effective date, as seen in Figure 1 [not shown]. Note that after October 2005, bankruptcy filings were lower than the previous two-year average. Discussions with

---

7. See Shepard (1984a). Several features of the 1978 Act made filing for bankruptcy relatively more attractive than in the past: (i) federal exemption levels were increased, (ii) the requirement that creditors must approve the repayment plan under Chapter 13 was removed, (iii) Chapter 13 provided for the discharge of some debts that could not be discharged under Chapter 7, and (iv) eligibility for Chapter 13 was expanded, thus allowing almost all individuals protection from creditors under Chapter 7.

8. The 2005 Act can be found at www.uscourts.gov/bankruptcy-courts/ abuseprotection.pdf. Various legal professionals in St. Louis and Memphis have commented to the author that the 2005 Act has many loopholes that result in minimal additional costs to consumers realtive to earlier bankruptcy laws.

various bankruptcy professionals reveal, however, that personal bankruptcy filings are again on the rise.

The Bankruptcy Boom: Cited Culprits

The primary cause of personal bankruptcy is a high level of consumer debt often coupled with an unexpected insolvency event, such as the loss of a job, a major medical expense not covered by insurance, divorce, or death of a spouse (Gropp, Scholz, and White, 1997; Buckley and Brinig, 1998; and Nelson, 1999). Lower- to middle-income individuals are more likely to file for bankruptcy in response to an insolvency event, given their relatively limited access to financial counseling and fewer and less-diversified financial resources. According to consumer economists' surveys, the typical bankruptcy filer is a blue collar, high school graduate who is the head of a household in the lower-middle income class, with heavy use of credit.[9] But, as mentioned earlier, this description of the average bankruptcy filer cannot by itself explain the rapid increase in personal bankruptcy filings that has occurred over the past 30 years.

It is unlikely that one event triggered the rise in bankruptcy filings. Rather, various economic and institutional changes have occurred that are likely contributors. Many of the changes discussed in this paper, such as the increased availability of credit, lower costs to filing for bankruptcy, decreased consumer savings, and increased consumer debt, do not necessarily cause bankruptcies, per se, but rather have made individuals more susceptible to negative income shocks, thus increasing the *chance of* bankruptcy.

Economic Factors. Personal bankruptcy filings per 1,000 persons in the United States from 1900 to 2005 are shown in Figure 2 [not shown].[10] Bankruptcy filings were relatively low

---

9. Shepard (1984b).
10. Data prior to 1960 was obtained from Hansen and Hansen (2006); for these years, it was assumed that "miscellaneous bankruptcies" reported in Hansen and Hansen were 60 percent corporate and 40 percent personal.

and steady from about 1900 to 1920. Filings then increased slightly during the 1920s and 1930s. World War II saw a marked drop in filings, likely the result of increased employment in support of the war effort. After the war, the number of filings increased and continued to do so into the 1960s. Two reasons for this rise were an increase in economic activity following World War II and the rise in federal and state transfer programs such as Medicare, welfare, and disability, which (i) may have created an incentive for individuals to be less financially responsible given the expanding government safety net or (ii) is reflective of generally poorer financial decision making by lower-income individuals.[11]

Corresponding with the dramatic change in bankruptcy filings since the early 1980s has been a marked decrease in consumer savings. For example, total saving as a percentage of income averaged nearly 10 percent in 1980 compared with 0.1 percent in the second quarter of 2005 (see Figure 3 [not shown]).[12] Although rising property values have likely led to a portfolio shift from traditional savings to investing in one's home, this latter option offers much less diversity, and thus higher risk, than traditional savings.

Consumer debt has increased dramatically over the past 30 years. Consumer debt service, which includes mortgage payments and personal debt (including credit cards), as a percentage of income increased from about 11 percent of per-

11. Visa USA, Inc. (1996) and Edmiston (2006).
12. The savngs rate referred to here is the difference between disposable personal income and current consumption divided by disposable personal income. This measure of the savings rate is from the Bureau of Economic Analysis' National Income and Product Accounts (NIPA). This measure of savings is not without criticism. For example, realized capital gains are excluded, whereas taxes on realized capital are included. Also, pension benefits are not included in personal income but contributions to pensions are deducted from personal income. Another measure of the savings rate is based on the flow of funds (FOF) by the Federal Reserve Board of Governors. This measure computes savings as the change in net wealth divided by disposable income. The FOF measure and the NIPA measure are quite different. The FOF savings rate averaged 11.2 percent between 1954 and 2006, and the NIPA measure averaged 6.9 percent over the same time period. Although producing different estimates of the savings rate, the two measures are correlated over time.

sonal income in 1980 to nearly 14 percent of income in the second quarter of 2005, as seen in Figure 3 [not shown]. Similarly, consumer financial obligations (a broader measure than consumer debt) as a percentage of income have increased since 1980, as seen in Figure 3 [not shown].[13] These statistics, combined with the saving statistics, reveal that Americans have been saving less and spending more (through debt) over the past 30 years, thus making individuals more susceptible to negative income shocks and thus more likely to file for bankruptcy.

The simultaneous spread of casino gambling and rising bankruptcy rates in the 1990s has been noted and studied for evidence of a causal relationship. Research has provided mixed results. The U.S. Treasury Department (1999), using data from 1962 to 1998 and applying an intervention model, found no measurable effect of gambling on personal bankruptcy rates in Mississippi and New Jersey. Expanding on the study performed by the Treasury Department, de la Viña and Bernstein (2002) examined county-level bankruptcy rates for the years 1988 to 1996. The authors found no relationship between casino gambling (available within a 50-mile radius) and bankruptcy.

Americans have been saving less and spending more (through debt) over the past 30 years, thus making individuals more susceptible to negative income shocks and thus more likely to file for bankruptcy.

Thalheimer and Ali (2004) examined personal bankruptcy rates over the period 1990 to 1997 in the riverboat gambling states of Iowa, Illinois, Missouri, and Mississippi. The authors found that access to casino gambling had no significant influ-

---

13. Financial obligations is a broader measure than consumer debt in that it considers automobile payments, rental payments, homeowners insurance, and property tax payments.

ence on personal bankruptcies. However, the authors did estimate that personal bankruptcy rates, on average, would have been 0.4 percent lower in the absence of casino gambling.

Finally, Barron, Staten, and Wilshusen (2002) found a small localized influence of casino gambling on bankruptcy. Using county-level data for the period 1993 to 1999, the authors found that casino gambling had a positive and significant influence on personal bankruptcy. They noted that, without gambling, counties with or adjacent to casinos would have had bankruptcy rates that were 5.4 percent lower in 1998.

Institutional Factors. The rise in personal bankruptcies in the 1920s and 1930s, along with growing corruption and legal challenges regarding corporate bankruptcy filings during the Great Depression, prompted passage of the Chandler Act in 1938. The Chandler Act created a host of new options for those filing for personal bankruptcy, such as alternatives to complete liquidation (e.g., a repayment plan) and a greater ability to file voluntary petitions. The bankruptcy reforms that resulted from the Chandler Act made personal bankruptcy filing relatively more attractive and less costly than in the past.

Although wealthier families are more likely to have a credit card than lower income families, their balances are a smaller percentage of their income.

An increased availability of consumer credit, especially in the form of credit cards, has occurred since the 1950s.[14] Although proprietary charge cards were available in the early 1900s, the use of these cards was traditionally limited to a single store. Also, many of these cards did not have the feature of revolving credit.[15] The first general purpose credit card (BankAmericard, now known as Visa) was introduced in 1966.

14. Sienkiewicz (2001).
15. Revolving credit is an agreement to lend a specific amount to a borrower and to allow that amount to be borrowed again once it has been repaid.

In 1970, only 16 percent of families had a credit card, compared with 82 percent of families in 2000.

Table 1 [not shown] shows statistics on credit card ownership and balances, broken down into family income categories for select years.[16] The top portion of the table reveals that credit card ownership by all income groups has increased over time, but that wealthier families are more likely to possess a credit card. For example, in 1970, only 2 percent of the lowest income families possessed a credit card, compared with 47 percent in 2003. But, in 1970, 33 percent of the highest income families possessed a credit card, compared with 99 percent in 2003.

Not surprisingly, higher income groups tend to have higher balances. However, the important measure is balance as a percentage of income—which reflects the *burden* of credit card debt. As seen in Table 1 [not shown], average credit card balances for the lowest income families are a greater percentage of family income than balances for wealthier families. In 1970, for example, credit card balances were about 5 percent of income for the lowest income families and less than 1 percent of income for the highest income families. In 2003, credit card balances were nearly 12 percent of income for the lowest income families and roughly 8.5 percent of income for the highest income families. Although wealthier families are more likely to have a credit card than lower income families, their balances are a smaller percentage of their income.

The late 1970s saw numerous legal changes that likely had an impact on bankruptcy filings. First, the Bankruptcy Reform Act of 1978 revamped bankruptcy practices set forth under the 1898 Act and the Chandler Act. Although the 1978 Act was passed in response to the rise in personal bankruptcies

[16] Data prior to 2003 were obtained from Durkin (2000). Data for 2003 were computed using data from the Survey of Consumer Finances (2004). "Lowest" is the upper range of the first quartile (about $25,000 in 2004), "middle" is the upper range of the third quartile (about $66,000 in 2004), and "highest" is the lowest range of the top 5 percent (about $174,000 in 2004). See www.census.gov/hhes/www/income/histinc/f01ar.html for a description of the family income distribution data.

during the 1960s, many provisions in the Act made it easier for both businesses and individuals to file for bankruptcy. Academic research on the effect of the Bankruptcy Reform Act of 1978 on subsequent bankruptcy filings is mixed, however. (Shepard, 1984a; and Domowitz and Eovaldi, 1993)

A second legal change in the late 1970s was a Supreme Court ruling in 1978 called the Marquette decision.[17] Prior to this time, many states had usury ceilings on credit card interest rates. The high inflation and interest rates of the late 1970s significantly reduced the earnings of credit card companies. As a result, credit card companies in states with relatively high interest rate ceilings attempted to solicit their credit cards to people living in states with lower interest rate ceilings—and still charge the higher interest rates.

Controversy over this practice culminated in the Supreme Court, which ruled that lenders in states with high interest rate ceilings could export those high rates to consumers residing in states with more restrictive interest rate ceilings. The result of this ruling was an expansion of credit card availability and a reduction in the average credit quality of card holders.

Another potential contributor to the rise in bankruptcy filings is the decrease in the social stigma associated with filing for bankruptcy.

The third legal change in the late 1970s was the Community Reinvestment Act (CRA), which was enacted in 1977 to encourage depository institutions to help meet the credit and financing needs of the community, especially low- to moderate-income communities.[18] Because the Act has increased credit flows to disadvantaged communities, it is possible that it also has increased the number of bankruptcy fil-

---

17. The actual case is Marquette National Bank v. First of Omaha Service Corp. See Ellis (1998) for a discussion.

18. See stlouisfed.org/community/about_cra.html for a discussion of the Community Reinvestment Act.

ings by lower income individuals. Research has suggested that the number of bankruptcies that result from CRA loans is, at most, 3 to 4 percent of overall bankruptcy filings.[19]

Although some minor legal changes to the Bankruptcy Code did occur in the 1980s, the next significant change was the Bankruptcy Reform Act of 1994. Each state has laws regarding the percentage of an individual's various assets that are exempt from creditors when that individual files for bankruptcy. These assets include insurance plans, pensions, personal property, and real estate (the homestead exemption). The federal government also sets exemption levels for these assets, and individuals may choose between using the federal exemption and their state's exemption (depending which is higher) if their state allows such a choice.[20] The 1994 Act increased federal personal property exemption levels, which in essence made it less costly for individuals to file for bankruptcy because they could now keep a greater percentage of their assets. Not surprisingly, personal filings increased roughly 17 percent between 1994 and 1995 in the states affected by the higher federal exemptions.

In addition to the legal changes that have occurred over the past several decades, another potential contributor to the rise in bankruptcy filings is the decrease in the social stigma associated with filing for bankruptcy. Although such a measure is largely unquantifiable, it is not unreasonable to suspect that filing for bankruptcy becomes less undesirable as more people declare bankruptcy. It is likely that the aforementioned legal and economic changes were greater causes of the initial rise in filings rates over the past 30 years, but the public's view of personal bankruptcy arguably would have become less negative as a greater percentage of the population had filed for bankruptcy.

19. See Gramlich (1999) www.federalreserve.gov/BoardDogs/speeches/1999/19990616 .htm.
20. The following states allow debtors to select the federal or state exemptions: AR, CT, HI, MA, MI, MN, NJ, NM, PA, RI, SC, TX, VT, WA, WY. See www.Bankruptcyinformation.com for detailed information on each state's bankruptcy laws and exemptions.

This section has discussed the institutional changes that are likely contributors to the rapid increase in personal bankruptcy filings: the rise in credit card usage and the relaxation of restrictions on interstate credit card provision; greater availability of credit to lower income individuals; decreased social stigma associated with bankruptcy filings; and changes to bankruptcy law that have made it less costly for individuals to file for bankruptcy.

Empirically disentangling the effect of each of the institutional changes on bankruptcy filings is quite difficult, however. As seen in Figure 2 [not shown], there is a marked break in the trend level of bankruptcy filings in the late 1970s and early 1980s—the period of time that corresponds with many of the legal changes that have been hypothesized to increase the rate of bankruptcy filings. Bankruptcy filings were regressed on a time trend for two periods: 1900 to 2005 and 1978 to 2005. Not surprisingly, empirical tests revealed that the coefficient on the 1978 to 2005 time trend variable was statistically greater than the coefficient on the overall sample period.[21] However, because many of these events occurred around the same period of time, it is difficult to determine the separate effects of each event on bankruptcy filings. Thus, it remains unclear whether all changes have had some effect on bankruptcy filings or the rapid rise is the result of only one or two events. . . .

References

Barro, Robert and Sala-i-Martin, Xavier. *Economic Growth.* New York: McGraw Hill, 1995.

Barron, John M.; Staten, Michael E. and Wilshusen, Stephanie M. "The Impact of Casino Gambling on Personal Bankruptcy Filing Rates." *Contemporary Economic Policy,* October 2002, *20*(4), pp. 440–55.

21. The coefficient (standard error) on Trend1900-2005 = 0.0086 (0.0012), and the coefficient (standard error) on Trend1978-2005 = 0.164 (0.0047).

Buckley, F.H. and Brinig, Margaret F. "The Bankruptcy Puzzle." *Journal of Legal Studies*, January 1998, *27*(1), pp. 187–207.

Carlino, Gerald and Mills, Leonard. "Convergence and the U.S. States: A Time Series Analysis." *Journal of Regional Science*, November 1996, *36*(4), pp. 597–616.

de la Viña, Lynda and Bernstein, David. "The Impact of Gambling on Personal Bankruptcy Rates." *Journal of Socio-Economics*, 2002, *31*(5), pp. 503–09.

Domowitz, Ian and Eovaldi, Thomas L. "The Impact of the Bankruptcy Reform Act of 1978 on Consumer Bankruptcy." *Journal of Law and Economics*, October 1993, *36*(2), pp. 803–35.

Durkin, Thomas. "Credit Cards: Use and Consumer Attitudes, 1970–2000." *Federal Reserve Bulletin*, September 2000, *86*(9), pp. 623–24.

Durlauf, Steven N. "Manifesto for a Growth Econometrics." *Journal of Econometrics*, January 2001, *100*(1), pp. 65–69.

Edmiston, Kelly D. "A New Perspective on Rising Nonbusiness Bankruptcy Filings Rates: Analyzing the Regional Factors." Federal Reserve Bank of Kansas City *Economic Review*, Second Quarter 2006, pp. 55–83.

Ellis, Diane. "The Effect of Consumer Interest Rate Deregulation on Credit Card Volumes, Charge-offs, and the Personal Bankruptcy Rate." *FDIC: Bank Trends*, March 1998, Number 98–05.

Fan, Wei and White, Michelle J. "Personal Bankruptcy and the Level of Entrepreneurial Activity." *Journal of Law and Economics*, October 2003, *46*(2), pp. 543–67.

Filer, Larry H. II and Fisher, Jonathan D. "The Consumption Effects Associated with Filing for Personal Bankruptcy." *Southern Economic Journal*, April 2005, *71*(4), pp. 837–54.

Fisher, Jonathan D. "Marital Status and the Decision to File for Personal Bankruptcy: A Duration Model Approach." *Journal of Economics and Finance*, Fall 2004, *28*(3), pp. 348–60.

Fisher, Jonathan D. "The Effect of Unemployment Benefits, Welfare Benefits, and Other Income on Personal Bankruptcy." *Contemporary Economic Policy*, October 2005, *23*(4), pp. 483–92.

Gramlich, Edward M. "A Policy in Lampman's Tradition: The Community Reinvestment Act." Remarks at the Second Annual Robert J. Lampman Memorial Lecture, University of Wisconsin, Madison, June 16, 1999.

Gropp, Reint; Scholz, John Karl and White, Michelle J. "Personal Bankruptcy and Credit Supply and Demand." *Quarterly Journal of Economics*, February 1997, *112*(1), pp. 217–51.

Hanson, Bradley and Hanson, Mary. "The Transformation of Bankruptcy in the United States." Working paper, University of Mary Washington, 2006.

Nelson, Jon P. "Consumer Bankruptcy and Chapter Choice: State Panel Evidence." *Contemporary Economic Policy*, October 1999, *17*(4), pp. 552–66.

Quah, Danny. "Empirical Cross-Section Dynamics in Economic Growth." *European Economic Review*, April 1993, *37*(2/3), pp. 426–34.

Shepard, Lawrence. "Personal Failures and the Bankruptcy Reform Act of 1978." *Journal of Law and Economics*, October 1984a, *27*(2), pp. 419–37.

Shepard, Lawrence. "Accounting for the Rise in Consumer Bankruptcy Rates in the United Status: A Preliminary Analysis of Aggregate Data (1945–1981)." *Journal of Consumer Affairs*, Winter 1984b, *18*(2), pp. 213–30.

Sienkiewicz, Stan. "Credit Cards and Payment Efficiency." Payment Card Center Discussion Paper 01–02. Federal Reserve Bank of Philadelphia, August 2001.

Skeel, David A., Jr. *Debt's Dominion: A History of Bankruptcy Law in America*. Princeton, NJ: Princeton University Press, 2001.

Survey of Consumer Finances, 2004. Board of Governors of the Federal Reserve System; www.federalreserve.gov/PUBS/oss/oss2/2004/scf2004home.html.

Thalheimer, Richard and Ali, Mukhtar M. "The Relationship of Pari-mutuel Wagering and Casino Gaming to Personal Bankruptcy." *Contemporary Economic Policy*, July 2004, *22*(3), pp. 420–32.

U.S. Treasury Department. "A Study of the Interaction of Gambling and Bankruptcy." Washington, DC: GPO, 1999.

Visa USA, Inc. "Consumer Bankruptcy: Causes and Implications." Visa Consumer Bankruptcy Reports, July 1996.

Webber, Don J; White, Paul and Allen, David O. "Income Convergence across U.S. States: An Analysis Using Measures of Concordance and Discordance," *Journal of Regional Science*, August 2005, *45*(3), pp. 565–89.

The Economic Policies
of the Federal Reserve Have
Encouraged Consumers
to Take on Too Much Debt

William Norman Grigg

William Norman Grigg has worked as an editor for The New American. *He also is the author of* America's Engineered Decline *and* Liberty in Eclipse: The Rise of the Homeland Security State.

They came before dawn on Friday morning, gathering in cities and towns across the nation in lines that snaked down city blocks. These anxious people weren't queueing up for tickets to see Coldplay or Big & Rich; instead, they were seeking to file bankruptcy before the advent of a new, more rigorous law on October 18 [2005].

"There have been huge spikes in filings all over the country," commented Nathalie Martin of the American Bankruptcy Institute (ABI) to the *Pittsburgh Business Times*. "In New Mexico, there have been almost as many filings the two months before [the new law] as in the entire year. There are huge, huge increases."

Many of the debtors thronging federal courthouses were single parents overwhelmed by unsupportable credit card balances and crushing mortgage payments. More than a few were well-paid professionals who had over-leveraged themselves during the recent Federal Reserve-created credit glut. Others were small businessmen whose ventures had failed. Donald Calairo, a Pennsylvania attorney who specializes in business bankruptcies, reported a 50 percent increase in filings in the

William Norman Grigg, "From Debt to Dispossession," *The New American*, November 28, 2005, pp. 21–25. Copyright © 2005 American Opinion Publishing Incorporated. Reproduced by permission.

two months leading up to the new law, the so-called Bankruptcy Abuse Prevention and Consumer Protection Act.

Several large corporations also raced to beat the clock. Delphi, an auto parts manufacturer that spun off from General Motors in 1999, filed for Chapter 11 bankruptcy protection on October 8. Delphi was joined by two ailing airlines, Delta and Northwest, who filed just ahead of the deadline. Under the new law, corporations filing for bankruptcy confront severe limits in the size of severance packages for top executives: the maximum amount cannot exceed 10 times the amount paid to non-executive employees.

Tens of millions of consumers will confront much steeper credit card payments just as it has become more difficult to liquidate outstanding household debt via bankruptcy.

A New Law Tightens Bankruptcy Rules

Obviously, people who take on debt should be morally and legally liable to pay it off, but the timing of this new law's implementation couldn't be worse. The new law imposes a "means test" based on cost of living guidelines composed by the Internal Revenue Service. Those found to have an above-average income are now barred from filing under Chapter 7, which permits debts to be expunged. They are now required to file under Chapter 13, which imposes a five-year repayment plan. Filers are also required to enter a professional credit counseling program within six months.

Facing intractable debts and rising household expenses, and concluding that bankruptcy was their inevitable destination, hordes of Americans decided to preempt the new law. In the week prior to the October 18 deadline, more than 103,000 bankruptcy petitions were filed (more than 20,000 per day), bringing the 2005 total up to 14.7 million—an increase of nearly 20 percent over 2004.

"We have never seen anything like this," commented St. Louis consumer bankruptcy attorney Barbara J. May to the *New York Times*. "We knew it would be an upswing, but this is pandemonium."

More Americans Are Exposed to Financial Ruin

"While the economy still seems to be pretty good, it doesn't take a lot to get people in trouble," observed ABI's scholar in residence, Nathalie Martin, to *The New American*. "Practically everybody is in debt, and it just takes one significant problem—such as sudden, unexpected healthcare cost—to drive people into bankruptcy. This is very troubling because there are at least four major developments converging right now" that threaten the financial ruin of millions of Americans.

The first of those developments, according to Professor Martin, is the new bankruptcy law itself, which "makes the process more costly and difficult for everyone." The second is a newly enacted federal regulation allowing credit card companies to double minimum payments; that measure went into effect at the same time as the new bankruptcy law. Taken in combination, this means that tens of millions of consumers will confront much steeper credit card payments just as it has become more difficult to liquidate outstanding household debt via bankruptcy.

Professor Martin also points out that both interest rates and the cost of living are rising, the latter reflecting this fall's spike in energy costs. (The federal government dishonestly computes the consumer price index in such a way that "core inflation" excludes increases in the price of food and energy.) And over the next three years, millions of Americans with adjustable rate mortgages (ARMs) will face ballooning mortgage payments.

"The ARMs are very, very scary," Martin remarks. "When they start going up we're likely to see another wave of bankruptcies, or maybe even people simply walking away from their homes and mortgages altogether. And this will obviously have a huge impact on our consumer economy at large, which has become dependent on the housing and mortgage industry."

"There's an almost schizoid quality to our economy and culture that has done some very significant damage," Martin continues. "The new bankruptcy law conveys the message that people need to be wiser in the way they spend their money, and more responsible in dealing with their credit and financial obligations. Yet at the same time the consumer is barraged with endless messages—many coming from political leaders and key financial figures—urging him to take equity out of his home to fuel the consumer economy. It's almost as if we have a social duty to spend money we don't have in order to help the general economy, rather than thinking and acting responsibly regarding our own household economies."

Many Consumers Bank on Home Equity

The "schizoid" economic message decried by Professor Martin was captured perfectly in comments made by outgoing Federal Reserve [Fed] Board Chairman Alan Greenspan in February 2004. After acknowledging that the Fed would soon start to raise interest rates. Greenspan urged homeowners who had refinanced to lower fixed rates to refinance to ARMs, whose rates could only be adjusted in one direction—up. While Greenspan's admonition was the purest lunacy, millions of Americans acted on it, most of them out of desperation.

Beginning in 1994, Greenspan's Fed has pumped money and credit into the economy. One result was the now-notorious "dot-com" bubble, which drove high-tech stocks into the stratosphere before the bubble exploded in 2000. After the 9/11 [2001 terrorist] attacks, the Fed opened another gusher of liquidity to keep the markets from collapsing. Since then, millions of homeowners have used their homes as ATMs, using creative mortgage financing to fund consumer spending and absorb high-interest credit card debt.

Many analysts have pointed out that this has created a housing and mortgage refinancing bubble that is even larger—and potentially more catastrophic—than the high-tech bubble. Greenspan himself, while refusing to admit that a national housing bubble exists, has conceded that there are "regional" bubbles, creating what he has called "froth" in the national housing and mortgage market. Rising interest rates and an escalating cost of living both threaten to prick the housing bubble, which would result in collapsing real estate prices.

This would leave millions of homeowners turned "upside down": they would be left with negative equity in their homes, steeply increasing mortgage payments, and relentlessly increasing household expenses. The collapse would also prove devastating to all of the industries that have fed on the housing market.

Millions of homeowners have used their homes as ATMs, using creative mortgage financing to fund consumer spending and absorb high-interest credit card debt.

Americans Are Not Prepared for an Economic Crisis

Not surprisingly, most Americans are utterly unprepared for a financial calamity of this magnitude.

"Personal savings—funds left over after expenses, excluding stocks, home equity, and other holdings that are less accessible than cash—are at lows not seen since the Great Depression," reported the November 1 [2005] *Atlanta Journal-Constitution.* "For every $1 of after-tax income in the third quarter, Americans spent $1.01 on average, according to figures released [on October 28] by the Bureau of Economic Analysis. That means households are spending more than they're taking in and making up for that deficit with credit card charges and home equity lines of credit."

Once again, this reflects the perverse economic priorities that have been fostered by the Fed. In recent years, the Fed has defined its mission as that of stimulating "aggregate demand" in order to keep the economy afloat. At the same time, Fed officials—prominent among them Ben Bernanke, Greenspan's designated successor as Fed chairman—have railed against what they call a "savings glut" in Asia, particularly China.

As Professor Martin observes, the tacit but unmistakable subtext of these policies is the assumption that Americans have a moral duty to spend, rather than save, and to take on as much debt as possible in order to do their part for the economy. Where Americans generations ago deferred gratification in order to save, Americans today are expected to defer payment in order to spend. And prior to February 2004, the Fed held interest rates at artificially low levels in order to stimulate consumer spending—home purchases, auto sales, big-ticket consumer items, promiscuous use of credit cards for incidental spending, even fast food purchases. And the consequences have been utterly predictable.

The Fed has defined its mission as that of stimulating
"aggregate demand" in order to keep the economy afloat.

In 2003, aggregate U.S. consumer debt reached a record high of $1.98 trillion, a figure that did not include mortgages. In the same year, the savings rate was a record low, 1.3 percent of disposable income. This combination yielded a phenomenon referred to by economics analyst M.P. Dunleavy as "survival debt"—the use of credit cards to make up income shortfalls in dealing with inflexible expenses, including taxes. Not surprisingly, household bankruptcies hit a record high in

2003 as well. All of this explains why millions were willing to act on Greenspan's insane advice to refinance to an ARM in February 2004, and stand to be utterly wiped out when balloon payments begin to come due.

Thus, there is every reason to believe that the frenzied bankruptcy filings this past October represent merely the first trickle of pebbles heralding an oncoming avalanche.

Fed Policies Send Mixed Messages

American consumers who blanch at the prices they pay at gas pumps and checkout lines would welcome falling consumer prices. But the central banking elite has defined deflation as a scourge, and inflation as the remedy. This was summarized quite tidily in the headline of a May 19, 2003 *Wall Street Journal* report: "Having Defeated Inflation, Fed Girds for New Foe: Falling Prices."

Thus the Fed openly set for itself the task of protecting high prices by undermining the purchasing power of the dollar. And by inducing consumers to tie their household economies to inflated real estate and stock market values, the banking cartel has them caught in a double-bind: a collapse in home prices will wipe them out immediately, while sustaining high prices through inflation will wipe them out incrementally.

Incoming Fed Chairman Ben Bernanke has been a member of the Fed's Board of Governors since 2002. He describes himself as "a Great Depression buff, the way some people are Civil War buffs. . . . To understand the Great Depression is the Holy Grail of macroeconomics." Like most of his peers in the Power Elite, the Harvard- and MIT [Massachusetts Institute of Technology]-educated Bernanke has drawn precisely the wrong lessons from the Great Depression, viewing it as a vindication of the idea that the Fed must stave off deflation at all costs.

The Fed Considers "Unconventional Means" to Combat Deflation

A 2002 meeting of the Fed Board of Governors, reported the *Financial Times*, examined "unconventional means" to pump up a deflating economy. An anonymous Fed official (most likely Bernanke) told the paper that "buying US equities" would be an example of such possible measures, and later said the Fed "could theoretically buy anything to pump money into the system," including "state and local debt, real estate and gold mines—*any asset.*" (Emphasis added.)

Bernanke elucidated his views in a November 21, 2002 address to the National Economists Club in Washington. Deflation "is always reversible under a flat money system," he pointed out, because dollars—unlike gold—can be created at whim. "Like gold, U.S. dollars have value only to the extent that they are strictly limited in supply. But the U.S. government has a technology, called a printing press (or, today, its electronic equivalent), that allows it to produce as many U.S. dollars as it wishes at essentially no cost. . . . We conclude that, under a paper-money system, a determined government can always generate higher spending and hence positive inflation."

That speech earned Bernanke the sobriquet "Helicopter Ben" for its casual endorsement of the idea—originally suggested in a sarcastic comment by [economist] Milton Friedman—that the Fed and federal government could stave off deflation by printing bales of money and dropping them randomly from helicopters. But the Fed "can inject money into the economy in still other ways," noted Bernanke. "For example, the Fed has the authority to buy foreign government debt, as well as domestic government debt. Potentially, this class of assets offers huge scope for Fed operations, as the quantity of foreign assets eligible for purchase by the Fed is several times the stock of U.S. government debt."

But the Fed could also buy up "a wide range of private assets," including corporate bonds, bank loans, and mortgages.

In order to hold deflation at bay—that is, to save the economy from a badly needed and long overdue fall in prices—the Fed under Bernanke may be prepared to create ever-depreciating dollars in sufficient quantity to buy everything in sight.

"There's no limit to what the Fed is prepared to do," commented investment analyst Richard Daughty of the Smith Consultant Group to *The New American*. "The only tool it has is inflation—creating money out of nothing. And Bernanke has explicitly stated that the Fed has the statutory means to use the money it creates to buy anything and everything, including stocks, bonds, houses, and raw land. It's entirely possible that someday we'll see the banking cartel literally owning everything—and Americans are *letting* this happen."

In order to hold deflation at bay . . . the Fed under Bernanke may be prepared to create ever-depreciating dollars in sufficient quantity to buy everything in sight.

Consumers Are Left with No Good Options

But as noted above, debt-laden American consumers have been manipulated into a position in which they have no good options, since either inflation or deflation would be devastating. "Deflation would be a disaster," comments Daughty. "If the grotesquely inflated stock market were to collapse to its real value, for instance, trillions of dollars would be wiped out—a far greater amount even than we saw evaporate when the dot-com bubble burst in 2000. The collapse of the housing market would be even more catastrophic, since the real estate bubble involves practically the entire banking system. And mortgage refinancing has been practically the only engine driving consumer spending. So the Fed, which created this impending catastrophe, will find widespread sympathy for its solution, which is to inflate the currency even more—despite the fact that historically, it's inflation that destroys a country, not deflation."

If the Fed acts on Bernanke's musings about fighting deflation by buying "a wide range of private assets," concludes Daughty, "we're headed for a 21st century version of feudalism, albeit a more humane variety than we've seen before. Our healthcare system will be better, for instance, and the serfs will enjoy amenities that weren't available to their antecedents. But the banks will own everything, and the rest of us will be serfs."

Some New Deal Tactics Were Really Fascist Policies

There are other possible avenues the Bernanke-led banking cartel might pursue. In his November 2002 address, Bernanke praised the actions taken by FDR [Franklin D. Roosevelt] during his first year in office, which included a "40 percent devaluation of the dollar against gold . . . enforced by a program of gold purchases and domestic money creation." In fact, that program entailed gold *confiscation*, as well as imposition of fascist controls on the economy in the name of fighting deflation.

In his memoirs, Frances Perkins, FDR's secretary of labor, described how the president's "Brain Trust" pored over the writings of Giovanni Gentile, the chief theoretician of Benito Mussolini's corporate state. Under the Italian Fascist regime, producers were forced into government-controlled cartels called *consortia*, through which wages and prices were set.

In May 1933, the first of FDR's New Deal "consortia" came into being with the passage of the Agricultural Adjustment Act (AAA). Among other provisions, that act "established acreage and production controls, paying farmers *not* to grow or raise wheat, corn, cotton, hogs, etc., and to plow under crops and destroy livestock," recalls Ralph Raico, a senior fellow at the Mises Institute. "The aim was explicitly to raise the prices of all farm commodities. The preposterous economic 'theory' behind this was that if prices and wages were jacked up, that would increase 'purchasing power,' which was the way to lift the country out of the Depression. In the two years of the AAA's existence, before the U.S. Supreme Court declared it to be unconstitutional, it distributed some $700 million to farmers to restrict production and destroy their crops, in an attempt to make food (and textiles) dearer for consumers. And *that* at a time when millions were going hungry."

The following month, Congress enacted the National Industrial Recovery Act (NIRA), setting up the National Recovery Administration (NRA). Its aim, observes Raico, "was nothing less than total control of American industry, again in order to raise prices and wages and hence 'purchasing power.'" The codes came to encompass an estimated 95 percent of American industry. Businesses found to be in substantial compliance with the myriad self-contradictory provisions were permitted to display the NRA's "Blue Eagle" symbol, sparing them further harassment by the agency's enforcement arm.

The Federal Reserve system, a nominally private banking cartel intimately joined with the federal government to control the monetary system and dominate the economy, is itself the most powerful fascist enterprise in existence.

Government Policies Restrict Free Enterprise

"May Almighty God have mercy on anyone who attempts to trifle with that bird?" exclaimed General Hugh S. Johnson, head of the NRA, capturing the militancy with which his bureaucratic shock troops persecuted businessmen who persisted in free market behavior by trying to price their goods and services competitively. Before the NIRA was ruled unconstitutional by the Supreme Court in 1935, the NRA storm troopers actually arrested and jailed a tailor for the supposed crime of offering better prices than Johnson's tailor.

Writing of the New Deal in his book *The Roosevelt Myth*, John T. Flynn summarized: "Liberals called it the Planned Economy. But it was and is fascism by whatever name it is known." Former President Herbert Hoover, whose interventionist policies exacerbated the Depression and laid the groundwork for FDR's fascist revolution, ruefully came to the same conclusion, observing in his memoirs "This stuff was pure fascism. . . . It was a remaking of Mussolini's 'corporate state.'"

Fascism, in the economic realm, is a corrupt fusion of centralized government and politically insulated private corporations. The Federal Reserve system, a nominally private banking cartel intimately joined with the federal government to control the monetary system and dominate the economy, is itself the most powerful fascist enterprise in existence, and its incoming chairman is an unabashed admirer of the most overtly fascist elements of FDR's program. While a revival of feudalism may not be in our immediate future, Bernanke's ascent may portend an accelerated descent into fascism instead.

Unexpected, Exorbitant Medical Bills Can Force Consumers into Bankruptcy

Dan Frosch

Dan Frosch has worked as a journalist for the San Gabriel Valley weekly section of the Los Angeles Times, The Source, *and the* Santa Fe Reporter. *His work also has appeared in* In These Times, AlterNet, VIBE, *and the* Washington City Paper.

Five long years ago, Rose Shaffer's life seemed sweet. A nurse since the early 1970s, Shaffer had spent most of her sixty years working at various Chicago hospitals, rising through the caregiver ranks and raising three kids. Now in the twilight of her career, she'd been hired as director of nursing at a home health agency in the suburb of Lombard [Illinois]. The position made Shaffer proud—she knew her salary could pay off the mortgage on her house a little sooner. At the time, her cousin Barack Obama was fast becoming a rising star in the Illinois State Senate.

Seven months into her new job, Shaffer suffered a heart attack, and an ambulance rushed her to Advocate South Suburban Hospital. Shaffer assumed she was automatically covered—health insurance was a given at her previous nursing jobs. She thought she'd filled out the proper forms. But she hadn't.

A week later, Shaffer received a bill from Advocate for the three days she'd been hospitalized. It was for $18,000. Shortly thereafter, Advocate began sending letters to Shaffer demanding payment. Then, a summons to appear in court was tossed on her porch. Advocate was suing her.

Shaffer was terrified and didn't show at her court date. She says she even received a letter from the Cook County Sheriff's Department, threatening arrest unless she appeared. Under pressure from Advocate and now behind on her mortgage payments, Shaffer filed for Chapter 13 bankruptcy in December 2002, which meant her debtors would garner a reduced portion of the money she owed.

"The hospital saved my life, but now they were trying to kill me," Shaffer says.

Medical-Related Bankruptcies Have Skyrocketed

Rose Shaffer's experience has become disquietingly common. Since 2000, Harvard associate medical professors Steffie Woolhandler and David Himmelstein, along with Harvard law professor Elizabeth Warren and Ohio University sociology and anthropology professor Deborah Thorne, have been compiling data on bankruptcies in the United States. Their study, published on February 2 [2005] by the medical policy journal *Health Affairs*, found that between 1981 and 2001, medical-related bankruptcies increased by 2,200 percent, an astonishing explosion in a relatively short period of time. This spike far outpaced the 360 percent growth in all personal bankruptcies during roughly the same period.

In addition, the study uncovered surprising information about the affected population. While poor, uninsured Americans have long been the most obvious victims of a defective healthcare system, it's the middle class that suffers most in this case, accounting for about 90 percent of all medical bankruptcies, says Warren.

"The people we found to be profoundly affected are not some distant underclass. They're the very heart of the middle class," Warren says. "These are educated Americans with decent jobs, homes and families. But one stumble, and they end up in complete financial collapse, wiped out by medical bills."

With so many middle-class American households potentially vulnerable, you might think politicians would seek a solution sensitive to their interests. Yet the momentum in Washington is in the opposite direction—toward bankruptcy "reform" that would make things worse for people who have been financially ruined by illness.

Until twenty-five years ago, filing for bankruptcy because of debts from a medical problem was virtually unheard of. In 1981, University of Texas law professors conducting bankruptcy research noticed that a handful of the debtors they were studying could never quite pay off their medical bills, but while these bills certainly didn't help, they weren't forcing people into bankruptcy.

The people we found to be profoundly affected are not some distant underclass. They're the very heart of the middle class.

Medical Debt Is a Leading Cause of Bankruptcy

Today, by contrast, medical-related debt is the second leading cause of personal bankruptcies, topped only by job loss. Edward Janger, a professor at Brooklyn Law School, gives two reasons for the change: First, there's been a dramatic rise in healthcare costs. In 2002 Americans paid an average of $5,440 in medical expenditures, up $419 from the previous year. A September 2004 study by Families USA found that 14.3 million Americans now hemorrhage more than a quarter of their earnings into healthcare costs.

Second, the past fifteen years have seen a tremendous spike in the number of Americans who either don't have health insurance or have such skeletal coverage they might as well have none—there are currently some 45 million uninsured Americans, a jump of 10 million since 1990.

"What you're seeing in the bankruptcy numbers is a function of the fact that we have a very thin social safety net in this country in terms of health care," Janger says.

The *Health Affairs* study, which looked specifically at a cross section of 1,771 bankruptcies filed in 2001, concluded that the average medical debtor was a 41-year-old homeowning woman, with children and at least some education. The study also found that a majority of middle-class debtors had health insurance both when they first grew sick and at the actual time they filed, another surprise. Insurance alone, it turns out, doesn't prevent medical bankruptcy, because it is often too porous to provide a real buffer against the financial burden of a serious illness.

"A lot of people were bankrupted because of co-payments, deductibles or uncovered services, which added up to thousands of dollars in bills," says Steffie Woolhandler.

Insurance alone ... doesn't prevent medical bankruptcy, because it is often too porous to provide a real buffer against the financial burden of a serious illness.

Illness and Job Loss Lead to a Swift Change of Fortune

The story of Judy and Phil Specht shows how quickly livelihoods and bank accounts can collapse in the shadow of an illness, even when people initially have health insurance. It also demonstrates how medical problems, when coupled with job loss, can be particularly devastating—many debtors grappled with medical debt and income loss simultaneously, according to the *Health Affairs* study.

In 2001 the Spechts were living comfortably in Albuquerque, New Mexico, having worked at solid jobs there for years—Judy at a Philips semiconductor factory and Phil as a maintenance man at a retirement community. Together, the Spechts were bringing in around $40,000, which in New Mexico was enough to make the $787 monthly mortgage payment on their new home and still have a little left. Lately, Phil hadn't been feeling great—his body ached more than usual—but the Spechts both had health coverage through their jobs. In their late 50s, they were near enough retirement to taste it. By 2002, though, Phil had grown worse, and after a series of tests, doctors diagnosed myeloplysplastic syndrome, a bone-marrow disease that can cause leukemia. Phil retired and began collecting $1,080 a month in Social Security disability payments.

"I still had a good paying job with insurance that could cover us both, so I thought we'd be OK," Judy says.

But when Philips started shuttering some of its New Mexico factories three months later, Judy was laid off. She quickly found a job working at another semiconductor company, but after five months she was axed again. Now desperate, Judy took a housecleaning job at near-minimum wage. It was all she could find.

Fortunately, the Spechts only paid $50 a month for Phil's visits to University of New Mexico [UNM] Hospital oncologists, thanks to UNM's charity care. But they had trouble affording the regular blood work Phil needed and the monthly $507 in prescription drug payments for both of them, climbing quickly because Judy developed high blood pressure, high cholesterol, acid reflux and an underactive thyroid—"stuff I hadn't experienced before this."

Exorbitant Medical Bills Force Tough Choices

To save money, Judy chopped her blood pressure and thyroid tablets in half, took the acid-reflux medication less often than prescribed and quit her cholesterol pills altogether. "I was left with a choice of my medication or a roof over our heads."

To afford Phil's medicine, the Spechts sold their furniture, some jewelry, and a camera. But by the end of 2003, $4,000 deep in medical debt and with $90,000 still left on their mortgage, the Spechts knew they couldn't hold on to their house any longer.

They hired a bankruptcy lawyer and filed for Chapter 7, freeing them from debt but eviscerating their credit for seven to ten years. The bank foreclosed on their mortgage, and the Spechts moved twice before settling in a cheap apartment for people over 55. Although they now participate in a new state program that offers drug discounts to elderly New Mexicans, the Spechts still owe $1,000 in medical bills; even after filing for bankruptcy, the couple continued to rack up bills until Judy finally landed a state job that gave her health coverage. The stress of the past three years has changed the Spechts forever. Judy describes the whole process as "frightening and humiliating."

I was left with a choice of my medication or a roof over our heads.

"We'd wanted to retire in that house. We were heartbroken," she says.

Lobbyists and Legislators Push for Tougher Bankruptcy Laws

The nightmare lived by the Spechts and other Americans could become even more harrowing if some members of Congress have their way. For years now, a powerful coalition of banks and credit-card companies has been lobbying Congress to make it harder to file for Chapter 7 bankruptcy, which cancels personal debt, in favor of Chapter 13, which involves paying back a portion over a period of time. As the number of personal bankruptcies has surged—from approximately 718,000 in 1990 to 1.54 million in 2004—banks and credit-card companies say, they've lost billions of dollars in canceled payments.

Republicans, and some Democrats, have long been pushing a bill that would create a means test for debtors who want to file for bankruptcy, preventing anyone who makes over the median income in their home state from filing for Chapter 7, but allowing them to file for Chapter 13. The idea, proponents say, is to make debtors take better care of their money.

Although the bill has failed in years past, Iowa's GOP [i.e., Republican,] Senator Chuck Grassley, buoyed by Republican Congressional gains and past support from moderate Democrats like minority leader Harry Reid, recently reintroduced the legislation. "People who have the ability to repay some or all of their debt should not be able to use bankruptcy as a financial planning tool so they get out of paying their debt scot-free while honest Americans who play by the rules have to foot the bill," says Grassley's spokesperson Jill Kozeny. Kozeny also notes that medical expenses would be deductible under the means test, and that adjustments to the test would be allowed if debtors show "special circumstances."

Jim Manley, Reid's communications director, says Reid will support the legislation, which he believes will force people to "take a measure of personal responsibility" for their financial affairs. Reid and some other Democrats will insist that it contain a provision preventing abortion clinic protesters from filing for bankruptcy to avoid paying legal fines (a practice that Reid, who is anti-choice, nonetheless opposes). Such a provision was added to the 2002 version of the bill in an attempt to give political cover to Democrats (including Senators Chuck Schumer and Hillary Clinton) who voted for it.

Some Lawmakers Oppose the Proposed Law

The legislation has nonetheless elicited some principled and vigorous Democratic opposition, from John Kerry, Jon Corzine, Dick Durbin, and Ted Kennedy, among others. The bill's critics argue that it will squeeze the lower middle class right out of the system. This demographic, they say, might still earn above their state's median income, deductions notwithstanding, yet may not be able to afford to hire an attorney to prove through litigation that their story is exceptional.

Moreover, says Elizabeth Warren, there's a good chance many middle-class debtors wouldn't even be able to make Chapter 13 repayments. Nearly two-thirds of those who file for Chapter 13 aren't able to pay up, leaving them vulnerable to creditors for years, she notes.

"The catastrophic problems which cause families to file for bankruptcy are not properly addressed by imposing greater requirements on people trying to get a fresh start," adds Ralph Mabey, co-chair of the legislation committee for the National Bankruptcy Conference, a national collective of bankruptcy experts that opposes the legislation.

Medical debtors, as the Health Affairs study shows, are suffering real hardship, which makes it hard to believe they are simply shirking their obligations and freeloading off the system, as Republican rhetoric suggests. In the two years before filing, 22 percent of families in the study went without food, 30 percent had a utility shut off, 61 percent went without important medical care and half failed to fill a doctor's prescription.

Nearly two-thirds of those who file for Chapter 13 aren't able to pay up, leaving them vulnerable to creditors for years.

"The bill is written against a template that everyone has overspent, including those with breast cancer, those fighting chronic illness, those who have lost children to cystic fibrosis or other terrible illnesses," says Warren. "It's like responding to a cholera outbreak by closing down the hospitals."

Lawsuits Challenge Health Care Collection Practices

Whatever happens politically, the fate of medical debtors will also be shaped by several cases now winding through the courts. Last summer [2004], law firms filed numerous lawsuits against nonprofit hospitals for overcharging uninsured patients, a practice that often contributes to bankruptcy. Attorney Richard Scruggs, who headed government lawsuits against big tobacco companies, is leading the federal effort.

On the state level, a class-action suit is pending in Illinois that involves Advocate, the source of Rose Shaffer's troubles. In November 2003 seven former patients filed the suit, charging Advocate with imposing discriminatory pricing (the number has since risen to seventeen). There is ample evidence for their claims. In March 2003 the Service Employees International Union [SEIU], the nation's largest healthcare union and an adversary of Advocate in organizing campaigns, released a study on the collection practices of fifty-nine Cook County hospitals. Advocate, which operates six hospitals in the county, ranked worst. According to SEIU, Advocate charged uninsured patients 139 percent more than their insured counterparts and was three times as likely to sue as other local hospitals. A month after the report's release, Advocate announced an increase in charity care for patients who couldn't pay. But for Rose Shaffer and others, it was too late. Later that year SEIU and Barack Obama brought Shaffer to Springfield to tell her story to the State Assembly.

"Advocate fails to provide automatic charity care discounts to the poor, and as a result the uninsured are still victimized by aggressive pricing and collections tactics," says Joseph Geevarghese, director of SEIU's Hospital Accountability Project. Advocate, which says it offers among the nation's most generous charity care, filed a motion to dismiss and a counterclaim against SEIU, accusing the union of defamation. The motion was denied last November [2004], but Advocate plans on refiling. The lawsuit will likely be tried this year [2005].

Still, University of North Carolina associate law professor Melissa Jacoby, who testified before Congress last summer on how hospital collection practices can cause bankruptcy, doesn't think litigation on its own will right the system. "Hospitals with the most egregious practices certainly should clean up their acts," she says, "but millions of people will still experience medical-related financial problems and their consequences, including debt collection and bankruptcy."

The only real cure for the medical bankruptcy epidemic ... is national health insurance—a system where coverage isn't linked to employment and medically necessary care is accessible to all without deductibles or copayments.

Bankruptcy Patterns Reveal a Host of Social Problems

Jay Westbrook, a University of Texas law professor who co-wrote the 1981 bankruptcy study, believes bankruptcy patterns are an indicator of other social problems—high unemployment, rising divorce rates (people often file for bankruptcy after a divorce) and, in this case, a crumbling healthcare system. "Bankruptcy occurs when there is a crisis. That's what it's there for," Westbrook says.

A study by the Center for Studying Health System Change shows that 20 million families struggled with medical debt in 2003. Federal projections suggest that out-of-pocket health expenses will rise at least until 2013. Elizabeth Warren and Steffie Woolhandler foresee medical bankruptcies continuing to climb as the uninsured population swells, overburdened hospitals aggressively collect to meet the bottom line, prescription drug prices increase and employers shift medical costs to employees.

The only real cure for the medical bankruptcy epidemic, according to Physicians for a National Health Program, is national health insurance—a system where coverage isn't linked to employment and medically necessary care is accessible to all without deductibles or copayments. If such sweeping reform seems a long way off, there are short-term fixes too. One would be to exempt medical debtors from any new laws restricting bankruptcies. "The bankruptcy courthouse doors must stay open for those who really need it," says Warren. Another worthwhile improvement, notes Henry Sommer, president of the National Association of Consumer Bankruptcy Attorneys, would be to better protect the homes of medical debtors; many states allow people only a small amount of home equity after they've gone bankrupt.

But even modest measures to protect medical debtors face an increasingly unforgiving environment. Although the recent litigation will likely force some hospitals to rethink collection practices, there's evidence they are finding other ways to reclaim money, like pushing debtors toward lenders and hospital-sponsored credit cards. And the bankruptcy reform pending in Congress could hurl many more middle-class Americans into lifelong debt.

Rose Shaffer, for one, is still reeling. She works two nursing jobs, seven days a week for nearly sixty hours, so she can make the monthly $2,088 in Chapter 13 payments she still owes. Advocate has yet to claim its portion, but Shaffer's credit is severely damaged and will be for the next decade. She's praying her eleven-year-old car will make it through the Chicago winter.

"Sometimes I would start crying. I wished I was dead, but I was too big a coward to kill myself," Shaffer says. "I never thought my life would end up like this."

Lenient Bankruptcy Standards Encourage Risk-Taking and Innovation

Aparna Mathur

Aparna Mathur is a research fellow at the American Enterprise Institute for Public Policy Research, a private, nonpartisan, not-for-profit institution dedicated to research and education on issues of government, politics, economics, and social welfare.

Entrepreneurs power the American economy. They enter and exit in a continuous, harmonious process that [economist] Joseph Schumpeter in 1942 called "creative destruction, ... the essential fact about capitalism." The toll is heavy. One-third of new businesses die in the first two years, and the majority fail to survive to year four. Despite such odds, the number of new entrants has been steadily increasing over time, and serial entrepreneurs thrive, resurfacing again and again. As a result, small businesses account for more than 95 percent of all enterprises in the United States, and close to 50 percent of all employment.

Much of the national policy debate about small businesses centers, naturally, on firms that survive. Taxes, healthcare costs, and capital subsidies are the concern of businesses that have more than minimal incomes, employees on their payrolls, and investment options. But what about firms that don't make it? How do we treat entrepreneurs who fail? The latest research suggests that this may be the most important question of all.

Over the years, America's personal bankruptcy system has served as a hedge against entrepreneurial failure. When busi-

Aparna Mathur, "Forgive Us Our Debts," *The American*, January/February 2007, pp. 86–88. Copyright © 2007 American Enterprise Institute for Public Policy Research. Reproduced with permission of *The American Enterprise*, a national magazine of Politics, Business, and Culture (TAEmag.com).

nesses fail, entrepreneurs can shield some of their assets from creditors by filing under Chapter 7 of the federal bankruptcy laws, the usual route for consumer filings. In fact, nearly 20 percent of all personal filings list business debts, and the value of business debts represents half the total liabilities of bankruptcy filers. But entrepreneurs are seldom the focus of debates about bankruptcy reform, which rarely distinguish consumers from small business owners.

Bankruptcy Can Give Entrepreneurs a Fresh Start

America's bankruptcy law is rooted in the "fresh start"—the idea that honest debtors experiencing a spot of bad luck, such as temporary job loss, illness, or divorce, are capable of putting the past behind them and moving on. This concept works especially well for owners of small businesses. By wiping out debts and pardoning failure, American bankruptcy gives the entrepreneur a chance to bounce back.

It's no surprise that these laws—seen as lenient not just by creditors but by much of the general public—have increasingly become a subject of debate in recent times. There is a growing fear that the system is too forgiving of debtors, and there is evidence that such criticism may be valid. The number of Americans seeking relief from creditors each year has more than doubled in the past decade to two million. This steady and rapid rise in bankruptcy filings has coincided with a generally robust economy (only one shallow and brief recession), leading to claims that filing for bankruptcy is simply a ploy to avoid paying debts.

Among the high-profile cases of abuse: O.J. Simpson, the pro-football player acquitted in a 1995 criminal trial of murdering his wife, moved to Florida to protect his extravagant home after losing a civil lawsuit two years later in California that required him to pay $33 million to the victims' families.

Under pressure from creditor groups, including banks and credit card companies, Congress in 2005 passed the Bankruptcy Abuse Prevention and Consumer Protection Act, which makes debtors jump through many more bureaucratic hoops to get relief. Signing the act, President [George W.] Bush said, "In recent years, too many people have abused the bankruptcy laws. They've walked away from debts even when they had the ability to repay them. This has made credit less affordable and less accessible."

The more a state forgives its debtors, the greater the entrepreneurial dynamism in that state.

But there is something important missing in the debate on bankruptcy: the implications of such legislation for entrepreneurial behavior.

Studies Confirm the Link Between Bankruptcy and Entrepreneurship

Does bankruptcy regulation affect entrepreneurship? My own research—along with that of Michelle J. White, professor of economics at the University of California at San Diego—answers with an unequivocal "yes." Studying variations in laws across the country, we find that the states that more extensively protect the assets of those filing for bankruptcy have more likely probabilities for business start-ups. Thus, the more a state forgives its debtors, the greater the entrepreneurial dynamism in that state.

Another recent study, by Thomas A. Garrett and Howard J. Wall of the Federal Reserve Bank of St. Louis, found that "the decision to become an entrepreneur is related to the homestead exemption"—or the proportion of the value of one's house that is protected from creditors in a bankruptcy. The researchers looked at the share of each state's working-age population composed of proprietors of businesses and found that the impact of lenient bankruptcy rules had a "statistically and economically significant" effect on entrepreneurship rates.

Entrepreneurship is often a process of trial and error. No one would accuse Henry Ford of being an unsuccessful entrepreneur. But Ford started two car companies that failed before he struck gold with Ford Motor Company.

Sometimes you fail for no fault of your own. If you know that your home and personal property will be protected no matter what the outcome of your venture, you are more likely to take the risk of starting a business in the first place—and to try again if you don't succeed. Our research found that states like Florida and Texas, with high personal bankruptcy exemptions, offer a better environment for businesses than Maryland or Virginia, with relatively low exemptions. The right to go bust is an insurance policy against financial disaster.

My work also indicates that states are less likely to see high entrepreneurship rates if their exemptions are lower than those of neighboring states. After all, entrepreneurs are free to move across state lines and take advantage of more lenient exemptions. Just as people vote with their feet by moving to states with lower taxes and better schools, entrepreneurs move to states with better bankruptcy regulations and better business conditions.

Bankruptcy Reform Must Consider the Role of Small Business

These findings warn that bankruptcy reform must proceed with care—and especially with a better understanding of the role bankruptcy plays for small businesses. But the 2005 law seems to be moving in the wrong direction. It introduced a slew of new provisions to make it harder for individuals to file for bankruptcy. For instance, only those with incomes below the state median can claim asset protection under Chapter 7; others must either devise a repayment plan out of future earnings or not file at all. Exemptions have been lowered for certain assets, and debtors need to undergo credit counseling prior to filing—a process that can be costly and, for many business owners, useless. A better approach would be to let creditors work through the market to ensure that debtors with bad credit history or risky entrepreneurial ventures are given loans at higher interest rates. This might lower the chances of default. Also, creditors could issue more secured debt to ensure repayment.

If entrepreneurs of failed businesses are denied debt discharge, they may take up safer wage and salary jobs rather than risk starting up a new venture. An unintended consequence of the legislation, therefore, may be the loss of another Henry Ford, Michael Dell, or Bill Gates. And lowering the level of asset protection provided to homes and personal property means even higher stakes for start-ups, deterring would-be entrepreneurs from risking creative destruction. My research shows a modest but unarguably negative impact from some of these changes on small-firm entry decisions.

History teaches us that entrepreneurship involves a process of learning and experimentation, and failure may well be a crucial part of that process.

A sad irony of the 2005 legislation is that, while many countries are learning from an American system that is seen widely as the world's most friendly to entrepreneurs, America seems not to be heeding its own lessons.

Unlike the U.S., many countries have found the notion of debt discharge alien, and only people who are deemed "hopelessly insolvent" are allowed to file for bankruptcy protection. In most cases, bankruptcy is imposed on the hapless borrower by creditors, assets are seized, and repayment of debt can extend over several years. Until recently, German statutes held the borrower liable for a firm's debts for nearly 30 years after filing. In Japan, business owners have been known to commit suicide rather than face the shame of a bankruptcy filing.

Do we really want to move toward systems where failure is feared and the entrepreneurial spirit takes a beating at every turn? Or do we want to tell our entrepreneurs that it's O.K. to fail? History teaches us that entrepreneurship involves a process of learning and experimentation, and failure may well be a crucial part of that process. As a society and an economy, our best asset may be our ability to accept and forgive. So each time we tighten our bankruptcy laws in response to the O.J. Simpsons of the world, we have to wonder if we are not, inadvertently, reducing America's dynamism.

One Should Explore All Options Before Declaring Bankruptcy

Ilana Polyak

Ilana Polyak is a business journalist based in New York City who writes about the financial industry, stock markets, and investments.

It was the daily flood of phone calls that finally did it. They became so overwhelming that Sabrina Young stopped answering her phone and resolved to give out her phone number to family, friends, and a few chosen others. As many as four creditors a day would call, demanding payment.

Young, a 52-year-old administrative assistant at Tennessee State University, had racked up more than $26,000 in debt and couldn't figure out how she was going to pay. Her list of financial obligations was long: A 2007 Pontiac G6 worth $18,000, medical bills of about $800, a computer for $1,500, a judgment of $6,000 for a car accident that Young was at fault for, and about $2,000 in credit card debt.

Making matters worse, Young's paycheck was now being garnished. She feared the garnishments would eat into her wages to the point where she wouldn't be able to make enough money to meet her basic needs. Young felt there was no other choice but to file for bankruptcy. Consequently, she filed for Chapter 13 protection in August [2008]. This type of bankruptcy allows Young to pay a reduced amount of her debts over five years. She'll pay $500 a month directly from her paycheck, including attorney fees. "I feel a lot of relief. Now, when someone calls I know it's not a creditor," says Young.

However, she says she regrets getting into this situation and wishes she had handled her finances differently.

Many have seen their wealth evaporate to the degree that bankruptcy seems like the best option, although in many cases it isn't.

Young is among the 850,000 who filed for bankruptcy last year [2007]—a number expected to exceed 1 million in 2008. "I've seen more people in the last year who have brought me the keys to their houses and cars saying, 'I just can't do it anymore,'" says O. Max Gardner III, a bankruptcy lawyer in Shelby, North Carolina.

With the subprime mortgage-sparked housing crisis, high unemployment rates, and shaky financial markets, many have seen their wealth evaporate to the degree that bankruptcy seems like the best option, although in many cases it isn't. Before you file, take the following into consideration:

Understanding the Basics of Bankruptcy Is Key

Bankruptcy has gotten more difficult—and expensive. It used to be that bankruptcy could be done on your own. But that has become significantly more difficult to do since the 2005 change in the bankruptcy law. First, there's a lot more paperwork involved. You'll most likely have to produce six months' worth of pay stubs, tax returns for four years, bills, bank statements, mortgage origination letters, and collection letters just to name a few.

You'll also have to pay more than in the past. According to the Government Accounting Office, the typical Chapter 7 bankruptcy involving a lawyer cost a minimum of $700 in 2005 and $1,000 two years later. Court fees also increased, and you'll now have to undergo two educational meetings with counselors. These sessions usually cost $50 to $75 each.

All of your debt will not magically disappear. Under Chapter 7 bankruptcy, which can take up to four months to complete, most of your debts are forgiven—with a few notable exceptions: student loans, alimony, child support, and some taxes. These debts must be paid in full.

Similarly, Chapter 13, which can take just a few weeks, will not discharge you of your debts, but will help you work out a plan to pay them off over the course of three to five years. Often, your debts will be significantly reduced, and you could end up paying just 20 cents on the dollar of what you owe.

You might have to sell your property. Each state has an exemption stating how much equity in your home you are allowed to keep. For example, the home equity exemption in New York is $50,000, but $350,000 in Nevada.

However, when it comes to Chapter 7 bankruptcy, anything above the exemption might result in you and your home parting ways: "If you have property above what you're allowed to keep, you might have to sell it," says Henry Sommer, president of the National Association of Consumer Bankruptcy Attorneys and head of the Consumer Bankruptcy Assistance Project, which handles bankruptcy cases on a pro bono basis in Philadelphia. So if you're in New York, and you have $100,000 equity in your home, you can keep only half of it. Chapter 13, which allows you to keep your home, might be a better choice if you've built up a lot of equity in your home and don't want to be forced to sell.

Your credit will take a hit. Credit scoring experts estimate that a bankruptcy filing can reduce your credit score by as much as 300 points. Unlike other negative marks on your report that take seven years to clear (such as a charged-off account), a bankruptcy filing stays on your report for 10 years before it can be removed.

Waiting too long to file can hurt you. While there's no exact formula for when to file, most experts agree that it should be prior to legal actions such as a car repossession or property foreclosure. A bankruptcy combined with repossession or foreclosure will mean that your credit will be in even worse shape.

"Because bankruptcy is so often portrayed as the option of last resort, people often wait way too long to consult an attorney," says Gerri Detweiler, adviser for Credit.com, a credit information Website, and co-author of *Stop Debt Collectors*. "In the meantime, they've drained their 401(k) to pay their debt. That doesn't help solve the problem; it just leaves them with nothing."

While there's no exact formula for when to file, most experts agree that it should be prior to legal actions such as a car repossession or property foreclosure.

Alternatives to Bankruptcy Are Available

If you haven't waited too long—meaning you're not at the point where your wages are about to be garnished and your home is in foreclosure—there might be other options.

- *Work out a deal with creditors.* With an increase in the number of people filing for bankruptcy, creditors might be more willing to work out a modification in your payment schedule.

- *Seek credit counseling.* Go for one session with a not-for-profit credit counselor to get some advice. Nothing will appear on your credit report. Beware of fraudulent credit counselors. Choose a not-for-profit agency that is accredited by either the National Federation for Credit Counseling or the Association of Independent Consumer Credit Counseling Agencies. You should not be required to pay high up-front fees for their services.

- *Meet with a bankruptcy attorney.* A bankruptcy lawyer might help you identify any unfair lending practices that can be challenged in court. "Bankruptcy attorneys should look at every claim that is there and see if you're dealing with an abusive creditor or debt collector," says Gardner. Most bankruptcy attorneys won't charge you for an initial consultation.

Determining Which Type of Bankruptcy Is Best

If you determine that filing is your only option, the next step is to decide which type of personal bankruptcy protection is best suited to your situation. In general, both Chapter 7 and Chapter 13 require these steps:

- *Prepare and file a petition.* Be honest about your assets and liabilities when completing these forms. If you find it too difficult to complete, consult an attorney.

- *Get credit counseling.* You must go through mandatory credit counseling with a court-approved counselor. A list of approved agencies can be found on the Department of Justice Website (*www.usdoj.gov*).

- *Meet with a trustee.* This is an accountant or a lawyer who will review your case to make sure all paperwork is filed correctly and collect any property that will be transferred to the court. In a Chapter 13 filing, the trustee is responsible for arranging your payment schedule.

- *Complete a debt education course.* You may complete this course only after you have filed for bankruptcy. But you must obtain a certificate of completion for it before you can receive an order of discharge. A list of approved educators can be obtained from the Department of Justice Website at *www.usdoj.gov/ust.*

Organizations to Contact

The editors have compiled the following list of organizations concerned with the issues debated in this book. The descriptions are derived from materials provided by the organizations. All have publications or information available for interested readers. The list was compiled on the date of publication of the present volume; names, addresses, and phone numbers may change. Be aware that many organizations take several weeks or longer to respond to inquiries, so allow as much time as possible.

American Bankruptcy Institute (ABI)
44 Canal Center Plaza, Suite 400, Alexandria, VA   22314
(703) 739-0800
e-mail: support@abiworld.org
Web site: www.abiworld.org

The American Bankruptcy Institute is a multi-disciplinary, nonpartisan organization committed to advancing research and education on matters related to insolvency. Its professional membership is composed of attorneys, accountants, judges, lenders, academics, credit professionals, and many others. ABI offers access to its consumer bankruptcy resources for a fee in an online Consumer Bankruptcy Center database. The organization also publishes the *ABI Journal*, the *ABI Law Review*, newsletters, and cases studies.

American Enterprise Institute for Public Policy Research (AEI)
1150 17th St. NW, Washington, DC   20036
(202) 862-5800 • fax: (202) 862-7177
Web site: www.aei.org

The American Enterprise Institute for Public Policy Research is a private, nonpartisan, nonprofit institution dedicated to research and education on issues of government, politics, economics, and social welfare. AEI's program on financial services covers accounting; banking; insurance, securities, and futures regulation; corporate governance; and consumer finance. AEI's financial services publications include "Unfree to Choose: The Administration's Consumer Financial Protection Agency," "Regulation without Reason: The Group of Thirty Report," and "What Should Society Want from Corporate Governance?"

Americans for Fairness in Lending (AFFIL)

7 Winthrop Sq., 4th Fl., Boston, MA   02110
(617) 841-8000
e-mail: info@affil.org
Web site: www.affil.org

Americans for Fairness in Lending is dedicated to reforming the lending industry in order to protect Americans' financial assets. AFFIL works to educate and advocate for American consumers and small businesses. In addition to a regularly updated blog, AFFIL's Web site offers opinion statements about lending practices, including "Credit Card Law's Effect on People Under 21" and "A New Era for Credit Cards."

Center for American Progress (CAP)

1333 H St. NW, 10th Fl., Washington, DC   20005
(202) 682-1611 • fax: (202) 682-1867
e-mail: progress@americanprogress.org
Web site: www.americanprogress.org

The Center for American Progress is a think tank dedicated to improving the lives of Americans through ideas and action. CAP combines policy ideas with a modern communications platform to help shape the U.S. national debate and challenge conservative philosophy. In a core focus area that addresses the economy, CAP concentrates on such topics as markets and regulation, credit and debt, the global economy, housing, and more. The organization's publications that concentrate on economic issues include "Putting Credit Card Debt on Notice," "Card Sharks," and "What Bank Mergers Mean for Credit Cards."

Center for Responsible Lending (CRL)

302 W Main St., Durham, NC   27701

(919) 313-8500

Web site: www.responsiblelending.org

The Center for Responsible Lending is a nonprofit, nonpartisan research and policy organization dedicated to protecting homeownership and family wealth by working to eliminate abusive financial practices. CRL has conducted or commissioned studies on predatory lending practices and the impact of state laws that protect borrowers. It also publishes many resources for consumers, including fact sheets on payday loans, overdraft loans, and mortgages.

Consumer Action

221 Main St., Suite 480, San Francisco, CA   94105

(415) 777-9635 • fax: (415) 777-5267

Web site: www.consumer-action.org

Consumer Action is a nonprofit, membership-based organization that was founded in San Francisco in 1971. During its more than three decades, Consumer Action has continued to serve consumers nationwide by advancing consumer rights and publishing educational materials in multiple languages. Among its many publications, several focus on debt, such as "Debt Consolidation: Is It for You?" and "Families and Credit Cards."

Consumer Federation of America (CFA)

1620 I St. NW, Suite 200, Washington, DC   20006

(202) 387-6121

e-mail: cfa@consumerfed.org

Web site: www.consumerfed.org

Since 1968, the Consumer Federation of America has gathered facts, analyzed issues, and disseminated information to the public, policy makers, and rest of the consumer movement. In addition to original studies, the CFA regularly publishes brochures and fact sheets available free to the public, including "Building Wealth Not Debt," "Managing Your Debts," and "Your Credit Score."

Consumers Union (CU)

101 Truman Ave., Yonkers, NY   10703-1057
(914) 378-2000
Web site: www.consumersunion.org

The Consumers Union is an independent, nonprofit organization dedicated to working for a fair, just, and safe marketplace for all consumers. The organization strives to change legislation and the marketplace to favor the consumer interest. CU publishes the monthly periodical, *Consumer Reports*, and two newsletters, *Consumer Reports on Health* and *Consumer Reports Money Advisor*.

Demos

220 Fifth Ave., 5th Fl., New York, NY   10001
(212) 633-1405 • fax: (212) 633-2015
e-mail: info@demos.org
Web site: www.demos.org

Demos is a nonpartisan public policy research and advocacy organization founded in 2000. One of the organization's core advocacy initiatives is the Economic Opportunity Program, which focuses on the economic insecurity and inequality that affects American society. The program offers analysis and policy proposals designed to provide new opportunities for young adults and financially strapped families seeking to achieve economic security. Demos publishes numerous books, reports, and briefing papers. Those that address consumer debt include "The Plastic Safety Net; How Households Are Coping in a Fragile Economy," "Borrowing to Make Ends Meet: The Rapid Growth of Credit Card Debt in America," and *Strapped: Why America's 20- and 30-Somethings Can't Get Ahead.*

Federal Deposit Insurance Corporation (FDIC)

550 17th St. NW, Washington, DC   20429
(877) 275-3342
e-mail: publicinfo@ftc.gov
Web site: www.fdic.gov

The Federal Deposit Insurance Corporation is an independent governmental agency committed to maintaining stability and public confidence in the nation's financial system by insuring deposits; examining and supervising financial institutions for safety, soundness, and consumer protection; and managing receiverships. As part of its overall mission, the FDIC supports a consumer protection initiative that provides resources to educate and protect consumers, revitalize communities, and promote compliance with government regulations and fair lending laws. The FDIC publishes several alerts related to consumer spending and debt management, including "Credit Cards: New Law Protects Consumers from Surprise Fees, Rate Increases and Other Penalties," "Managing Your Money in Good Times and Bad," and "Take Charge of Your Credit Cards."

Federal Trade Commission (FTC)

600 Pennsylvania Ave. NW, Washington, DC   20580
(877) 382-4357
Web site: www.ftc.gov

Founded in 1914, the Federal Trade Commission pursues vigorous and effective law enforcement and creates practical and plain-language educational programs for consumers and businesses. The FTC also administers a wide variety of consumer protection laws, including the Telemarketing Sales Rule, the Pay-Per-Call Rule, and the Equal Credit Opportunity Act. In addition to an annual "Performance and Accountability Report," the FTC regularly publishes consumer protection materials, including "Credit and Your Consumer Rights" and "Knee Deep in Debt."

National Association of Consumer Bankruptcy Attorneys (NACBA)

2300 M St., Suite 800, Washington, DC   20037
Web site: www.nacba.org

Founded in 1992, the National Association of Consumer Bankruptcy Attorneys is a national organization dedicated to serving the needs of consumer bankruptcy attorneys and protecting the rights of consumer debtors in bankruptcy. The NACBA is composed of more than 4,000 members located in all fifty states and Puerto Rico. NACBA files amicus briefs in selected appellate and Supreme Court cases that could significantly impact consumer bankruptcy rights. Many of these briefs are available on the NACBA Web site.

National Consumer Law Center (NCLC)

7 Winthrop Sq., Boston, MA   02110-1245
(617) 542-8010 • fax: (617) 542-8028
e-mail: consumerlaw@nclc.org
Web site: www.consumerlaw.org

The National Consumer Law Center is an organization dedicated to helping consumers, their advocates, and public policy makers use consumer laws on behalf of low-income and vulnerable Americans seeking economic justice. A top priority for NCLC is providing support on issues involving consumer fraud, debt collection, consumer finance, energy assistance programs, predatory lending, and sustainable homeownership programs. The NCLC publishes several titles for consumers, including *Surviving Debt* and *Foreclosure Prevention Counseling: Preserving the American Dream.*

National Foundation for Credit Counseling (NFCC)

801 Roeder Rd., Suite 900, Silver Spring, MD   20910
(800) 388-2227
Web site: www.nfcc.org

Founded in 1951, the National Foundation for Credit Counseling promotes a public agenda for achieving and maintaining financially responsible behavior. Its member counselors are committed to delivering financial education and counseling services to millions of Americans. Its publications include *Better Fortunes: Control Your Money. Control Your Life, More Than One Way Out: Personal Bankruptcy Consequences and Alternatives,* and *Live a Richer Life: A Roadmap to Personal Financial Health Following Bankruptcy.*

Project on Student Debt

2054 University Ave., Suite 500, Berkeley, CA   94704
(510) 559-9509
e-mail: info@projectonstudentdebt.org
Web site: www.projectonstudentdebt.org

The Project on Student Debt works to increase public awareness of the circumstances surrounding the need to borrow funds to pay for higher education and the implications that this necessity has for families, the economy, and society. Recognizing that loans play a critical role in making college possible, the Project is committed to identifying cost-effective solutions that expand educational opportunity, protect family financial security, and advance economic competitiveness. Its publications include "Denied: Community College Students Lack Access to Affordable Loans," "Private Loans: Facts and Trends," and "Quick Facts about Student Debt."

Bibliography

Books

Sumit Agarwal and Brent W. Ambrose, eds.
Household Credit Usage: Personal Debt and Mortgages. New York: Palgrave Macmillan, 2007.

American Bar Association
The American Bar Association Guide to Credit & Bankruptcy. New York: Random House Reference, 2006.

Giuseppe Bertola, Richard Disney, and Charles Grant, eds.
The Economics of Consumer Credit. Cambridge, MA: MIT Press, 2006.

Dawn Burton
Credit and Consumer Society. London, UK: Routledge, 2008.

Alan Collinge
The Student Loan Scam: The Most Oppressive Debt in U.S. History, and How We Can Fight Back. Boston: Beacon Press, 2009.

Stephen Elias
The New Bankruptcy: Will It Work for You? Berkeley, CA: Nolo Press, 2006.

David S. Evans and Richard Schmalensee
Paying with Plastic: The Digital Revolution in Buying and Borrowing. Cambridge, MA: MIT Press, 2005.

Steven Finlay
Consumer Credit Fundamentals. Basingstoke, UK: Palgrave Macmillan, 2005.

Anya Kamenetz   *Generation Debt: How Our Future*
                    Was Sold Out for Student Loans,
                    Credit Cards, Bad Jobs, No Benefits,
                    and Tax Cuts for Rich Geezers—And
                    How to Fight Back. New York:
                    Riverhead Books, 2007.

Robin Leonard   *Bankruptcy: Is It the Right Solution to*
                    Your Debt Problems? Berkeley, CA:
                    Nolo Press, 2004.

Robin Leonard   *Money Troubles: Debt, Credit, and*
and John Lamb   *Bankruptcy.* Berkeley, CA: Nolo Press,
                    2009.

Ronald J. Mann   *Charging Ahead: The Growth and*
                    Regulation of Payment Card Markets.
                    Cambridge, UK: Cambridge
                    University Press, 2006.

Christopher L.   *Taming the Sharks: Towards a Cure*
Peterson   *for the High-Cost Credit Market.*
                    Akron, OH: University of Akron
                    Press, 2004.

James D. Scurlock   *Maxed Out: Hard Times, Easy Credit,*
                    and the Era of Predatory Lenders.
                    New York: Scribner, 2007.

Garrett Sutton   *The ABC's of Getting out of Debt:*
                    Turn Bad Debt into Good Debt and
                    Bad Credit into Good Credit. New
                    York: Warner Business Books, 2004.

Stuart Vyse   *Going Broke: Why Americans Can't*
                    Hold on to Their Money. Oxford, UK:
                    Oxford University Press, 2008.

Elizabeth Warren and Amelia Tyagi	*All Your Worth: The Ultimate Lifetime Money Plan.* New York: Free Press, 2005.
Liz Pulliam Weston	*Deal with Your Debt: The Right Way to Manage Your Bills and Pay Off What You Owe.* Upper Saddle River, NJ: Pearson Prentice Hall, 2006.
Brett Williams	*Debt for Sale: A Social History of the Credit Trap.* Philadelphia: University of Pennsylvania Press, 2004.

Periodicals

Douglas Akers, Jay Golter, Brian Lamm, and Martha Solt	"Overview of Recent Developments in the Credit Card Industry," *FDIC Banking Review*, 2005.
Rob Baedeker	"The Paradox of Thrift," *San Francisco Chronicle*, December 22, 2008.
Rachel Beck	"Consumer Debt Defaults Loom Large," *Chicago Tribune*, September 11, 2008.
David O. Beim	"It's All About Debt," *Forbes*, March 19, 2009.
Tara Siegel Bernard and Jenny Anderson	"Downturn Drags More Consumers into Bankruptcy," *New York Times*, November 16, 2008.
Billie Ann Brotman	"The Relationship Between Medical Care Costs and Personal Bankruptcy," *Journal of Health Care Finance*, 2006.

Laura Cohn	"The Bankruptcy Solution," *Kiplinger's Personal Finance*, May 2009.
James Edmund Datri and Ivan L. Kallick	"Bankruptcy Bill Will Make Broken System Fair," *American Banker*, March 11, 2005.
Arthur Epstein	"Bad Times Are Good for Debt Collectors," *Business Week Online*, April 11, 2008.
José A. Garcia	"Borrowing to Make Ends Meet: The Rise of Credit Card Debt in America," *Demos*, 2007.
Kelli B. Grant	"Being Debt-Free Isn't Always All It's Cracked Up to Be," *SmartMoney*, January 24, 2007.
David U. Himmelstein, Elizabeth Warren, Deborah Thorne, and Steffie Woolhandler	"Market Watch: Illness and Injury as Contributors to Bankruptcy," *Health Affairs*, February 2, 2005.
Zachary Karabell	"We've Still Got Room to Spend," *Newsweek*, February 23, 2009.
Barbara Kiviat	"The Real Problem with Credit Cards: The Cardholders," *Time*, May 12, 2009.
Ron Lieber	"One Thing You Can Control: Your Credit Score," *New York Times*, October 11, 2008.

Joshua Lipton — "Choking on Credit Card Debt," *Forbes*, September 12, 2008.

Jeff Merkley — "Credit Card Reform Helps Economy," *Statesman Journal* (OR), August 30, 2009.

Gretchen Morgenson — "Given a Shovel, Americans Dig Deeper into Debt," *New York Times*, July 20, 2008.

Janet Novack — "Protection Time," *Forbes*, June 6, 2005.

PR Newswire — "Paying for College: Being Smart about Private Student Loans," July 30, 2008.

Walter V. Robinson and Beth Healy — "Debt Collectors Hunt the Innocent," *Boston Globe*, September 13, 2006.

Robert H. Scott III — "Bankruptcy Abuse Prevention and Consumer Protection Act of 2005: How the Credit Card Industry's Perseverance Paid Off," *Journal of Economic Issues*, December 2007.

Jessica Silver-Greenberg — "The Next Meltdown: Credit Card Debt," *Business Week*, October 9, 2008.

Darrell Smith — "As Filings Soar, So Does Bankruptcy's Personal Toll," *Sacramento Bee* (CA), May 8, 2008.

Brad Tuttle — "Credit Card Reform: While One Hand Gives, the Other Adds Fees," *Time*, August 20, 2009.

Erica Williams   "The Young and the Indebted,"
                      Center for American Progress, July 2,
                      2008. www.americanprogress.org.

Mike Woelflein   "'Payday' Loans," *The Officer*, March
                      2005.

Edward A.   "Getting Out of Debt and the New
Zurndorfer   Bankruptcy Law," *Federal Employees
                      News Digest*, March 15, 2007.

Index